CAPRIAL'S SEASONAL KITCHEN

CAPRIAL'S

SEASONAL KITCHEN

An Innovative Chef's
Menus and Recipes
for Easy Home Cooking

CAPRIAL PENCE

Alaska Northwest Books™
Anchorage • Seattle

My thanks . . .

To Fullers restaurant and the Seattle Sheraton Hotel and Towers,
for giving me the freedom to be creative.

To Dennis Chun, for allowing me to include his wonderful
Chocolate Swirl Bread Pudding.

To my husband, John, most of all, for putting up with
the long hours I put into this book and for taking care of me.

To my parents, for giving me the encouragement and love
to be the best I could be at whatever I wanted to do.

Library of Congress Cataloging-in-Publication Data
Pence, Caprial.
    [Seasonal kitchen]
    Caprial's seasonal kitchen : an innovative chef's menus and
  recipes for easy home cooking / by Caprial Pence.
        p.   cm.
    ISBN 0-88240-417-2 (hardbound) — ISBN 0-88240-418-0 (softbound)
    1. Cookery, American—Pacific Northwest style.   2. menus.
  I. Title.   II. Title: Seasonal kitchen.
  TX715.2.P32P46   1991
  641.59795—dc20   91-3274
                                                                      CIP

Edited by Andrea Jarvela and Marlene Blessing
Designed by Kate L. Thompson and Alice Merrill Brown
Illustrated by Robert Williamson
Cover photograph by Jim Mears; Food styling by Phyllis Bogard

Alaska Northwest Books™
A division of GTE Discovery Publications, Inc.
22026 20th Avenue S.E.
Bothell, Washington 98021

Printed in U.S.A. on acid-free paper

For Alex
The best thing John and I ever cooked up!

Contents

Contents

SUMMER

BASIC RECIPES

Introduction

THE PACIFIC NORTHWEST IS A wonderful place to live. Besides being a native—I was born in Pasco, Washington, and grew up in Portland, Oregon—I returned here after graduating from cooking school in upstate New York because the Northwest offered such an abundance of both natural beauty and outstanding local foods to cook with. I wrote this book because I wanted to convey my love of the Pacific Northwest, to pay tribute to the fresh, delicious foods that have inspired my approach to cooking, and to teach people you don't have to be a chef to cook wonderful meals at home. This book is not designed just for Northwesterners, however. It offers a concept and recipes that can be used in any region of the country. When following these recipes, try to use ingredients that are local and create your own regional variations.

The first place I was ever exposed to using local products almost exclusively is Fullers restaurant, in the Seattle Sheraton Hotel, where I am the chef. Here, small farmers and foragers often come through the back door of the restaurant to sell us their products. We believe it is just good common sense and one of the keys to great cooking to use as many ingredients as possible from our own area—the closer the source, the fresher the product. This approach carries over into my cooking at home. My husband, John—also a chef—and I often go to Seattle's Pike Place Market to shop for the best produce we can find for our dinners at home.

To take advantage of foods that are in season and at their peak of flavor, explore your city or town and the surrounding countryside for local fruits, vegetables, mushrooms, cheeses, seafood or poultry, wines—whatever your area produces. In the Northwest, oysters and mussels grow in Puget Sound, wild-caught or farmed salmon are available nearly year-round, there are many varieties of berries, and east of the Cascade Mountains are orchards of apples, peaches, apricots, and pears. There are also crisp vegetables, nuts, savory herbs, and several varieties of earthy wild mushrooms.

In addition to searching for fresh local products, bear in mind that food markets may apply the "fresh" label to many nonlocal foods. For example, there are many types of fish and shellfish flown into Seattle fish markets daily: salmon from Chile and Norway, swordfish and grouper from the East Coast, softshell crabs and oysters from Chesapeake Bay. With these and other foods, apply your own "freshness test." If you are buying seafood, sniff it; it should have a clean ocean smell, not a fishy odor, and should be free of blood spots or bruises. Produce should be crisp and green, not wilted or curling and yellow at the edges. Look for fruit without bruises, and berries without mold on the bottom of the carton.

A few words about freshness as it pertains to foods that you may eat raw. While most food and fish markets take great care to ensure that what you buy is safe to eat, some foods pose potential health hazards. You should be aware of possible health risks from shellfish eaten raw—such as oysters. The best way to be sure oysters are safe to eat is to ask whether they come from certified shellfish growing areas. If there are concerns about water quality in your area, check with your state health or environmental quality department to be assured you are buying shellfish free of contamination.

Raw eggs in fresh sauces or dressings, such as mayonnaise or aïoli, may also pose a health risk—Salmonella contamination. Because there is no clear knowledge as to the extent of the Salmonella problem, we all eat raw eggs at our own risk.

It's important to me that you enjoy your dinner party or brunch with your guests, and are not stuck in the kitchen. Great parties are those that are casual and look easy. To help you achieve this happy balance, many of my meals are designed so that you can make things ahead and have only minimal work to do at the last minute.

Some people believe that cooking fine food is difficult or even impossible for someone without training. Elegant meals aren't necessarily complicated and can be easy and enjoyable to prepare. It takes only a basic knowledge of cooking to prepare a wonderful brunch for six or a midnight New Year's Eve dinner for four if you use the best ingredients and are willing to be creative.

Expanding on a classic idea is how many chefs create wonderful new recipes. This is your chance to be innovative, too. Many of the recipes in this book offer suggestions for varying a dish slightly. Some also tell you how to substitute ingredients or correct mistakes—just in case. I hope these tips will give firmer footing to those who are little shaky in the kitchen and will inspire readers to treat recipes as beginnings for exciting new variations.

This book is organized by complete menus as a way to help you plan meals through the seasons. Each season has menus for dinners, lunches, and breakfasts, together with suggestions for a wine to serve with the meal. As with the individual recipes, give your imagination free rein and interchange dishes as you like, thus having the fun and satisfaction of personalizing the menus.

I hope this book brings you hours of pleasurable cooking and many wonderful meals with family and friends. So relax, and have a good time. Happy eating.

FALL

ROAST CHICKEN DINNER FOR 4

Wild Mushroom Phyllo Triangles

Roast Chicken with Sorrel Mussel Cream Sauce

Baked Apples with Walnuts and Dried Cherries

WINE SUGGESTION
Gordon Brothers Reserve Chardonnay

SOME OF THE PACIFIC NORTH-
west's foods are at their best in the fall. Mussels are fat and
succulent, newly harvested apples juicy and crisp, and my
favorite wild mushrooms—chanterelles—are available in local
markets from late August through Thanksgiving.

This dinner begins with an appetizer that combines the
earthy flavor of wild mushrooms with salty Kalamata olives,
tangy goat cheese, and sweet sun-dried tomatoes.

The nutty taste of chanterelles works especially well
with these distinctive ingredients, but you can use any wild
mushrooms, or even substitute domestic mushrooms. You
may want to try the smoky, rich-flavored morels, delicate and
mild oyster mushrooms, or shiitakes, which have a musty
flavor that is wonderful grilled. The phyllo triangles can be
stuffed, rolled, and frozen until ready to use. Tightly covered,
they will store for several months in the freezer.

Mussels and other shellfish become much more flavorful
as the seawater temperature cools during fall. In this recipe,
fall mussels are combined with lemony tart sorrel to produce
an elegant sauce to serve over simple roast chicken. The mussels are poached, then the poaching liquid is reduced to produce the sauce, and the mussels are used as garnish.

Fresh apples baked with a cherry and walnut stuffing
finish off this autumn meal. Apples are very versatile—they
can be used in everything from desserts to entree sauces. The
first of the new crop apples begin to arrive in September. For
this recipe, I like the tartness of Granny Smiths, a nice contrast to the sweet dried cherries. Walnuts and cream cheese
add texture and body to the filling, which can be made well in
advance. You can stuff and partially bake the apples ahead of
time, then finish baking just before dinner.

Wild Mushroom Phyllo Triangles

2 tablespoons unsalted butter
3 shallots, finely chopped
2 garlic cloves, finely chopped
2 cups sliced wild mushrooms (chanterelles, oyster
mushrooms, or shiitakes)
2 tablespoons minced sun-dried tomatoes
¼ cup chopped Kalamata olives
4 ounces soft mild goat cheese
Salt and pepper to taste
1 box phyllo dough
¼ cup melted unsalted butter

Preheat oven to 350 degrees.

Melt 2 tablespoons butter in a large sauté pan over medium heat. When the butter is hot, sauté the chopped shallots and garlic until you can smell the aroma. Add the mushrooms and sauté until tender. Remove from heat and mix in the sun-dried tomatoes, olives, and goat cheese. Salt and pepper to taste. Let cool.

Remove the phyllo dough from the box and cover with a damp cloth. (When preparing phyllo, work as rapidly as possible because the sheets dry out quickly.) Remove 2 sheets from under the cloth and brush lightly with melted butter. Fold the sheets lengthwise in thirds and brush again. Place one tablespoon of mushroom mixture on the bottom left-hand corner and fold it over to form a triangle. Continue to fold from the corner; it will resemble a folded flag. Brush top with more butter. Repeat process until all triangles are formed.

Place triangles on a baking sheet and bake until golden brown, about 10 minutes. Serve warm.

Makes about 8 large triangles (or more smaller ones)

20

Roast Chicken with Sorrel Mussel Cream Sauce

Sauce

1 cup white wine
2 shallots, finely chopped
3 garlic cloves, finely chopped
½ pound mussels, cleaned and debearded
1 pint heavy cream
1 teaspoon lemon juice
1 tablespoon chopped fresh sorrel leaves
Salt and pepper to taste

Chickens

2 2-pound, whole roasting chickens
1 teaspoon garlic powder
1 teaspoon paprika
Salt and pepper to taste

Sorrel sprigs for garnish

Preheat oven to 375 degrees.

To prepare the sauce: Place wine, shallots, garlic, and cleaned mussels in a medium-size, covered saucepan. Steam over high heat until the mussels open (about 3 to 5 minutes). Remove from heat, transfer the mussels to a separate dish, and set aside. Return the saucepan to high heat and reduce the liquid by half. Add the cream and reduce again over high heat until thickened. Season with lemon juice, sorrel, salt and pepper. Keep the sauce warm while you prepare the chicken.

To roast the chickens: Rinse the chickens and place in a large roasting pan. Season inside and out with garlic powder, paprika, salt, and pepper. Roast about 1 hour or until done. To test for doneness, stick a leg joint with a knife. The juices should run clear.

Remove the legs from the chicken and slice the breast, arranging breast meat and a leg on each plate. Pour sauce over the meat and garnish with the steamed mussels and a sprig of sorrel.

Serves 4

NOTE: To thoroughly clean the mussels, scrub under cold running water and firmly pull out the beard, or byssus threads.

Baked Apples with Walnuts and Dried Cherries

¼ cup dried cherries (Chukar)
¼ cup toasted chopped walnuts
½ cup cream cheese
¼ cup sugar
1 egg
½ teaspoon vanilla
½ teaspoon cinnamon
¼ teaspoon allspice
¼ teaspoon nutmeg
4 medium Granny Smith apples, peeled and cored

Whipped cream or vanilla ice cream (optional)

Preheat oven to 350 degrees.

In a food processor fitted with a metal blade, coarsely grind the cherries and walnuts. Add the cream cheese and incorporate well. Mix in the sugar and egg, then add vanilla and spices. (Make sure during this process to scrape down the sides of the food processor bowl several times.) Remove from the processor and reserve.

Using a pastry bag fitted with a plain tube, pipe the cherry and walnut filling into each hollowed-out apple. Set on doubled baking sheets and cover with foil, or place in a covered dutch oven. Bake until apples are soft, about 40 minutes depending on the size of the apples.

Serve with whipped cream or vanilla ice cream.

Serves 4

NOTE: If you prefer, you can bake the apples with the peel left on.

23

POACHED SALMON DINNER FOR 6

Chilled Prawns with Balsamic Mustard Aïoli

Poached Salmon with Chanterelle Cream Sauce

Strawberry Profiteroles
with Orange Caramel Sauce

WINE SUGGESTION
Chateau Benoit Pinot Noir

THIS ELEGANT FALL DINNER makes the most of two popular types of seafood, prawns and salmon. The meal begins with Alaskan spotted prawns, served with a tangy, garlic aïoli. A dab of aïoli, with its blend of sweet, sherrylike balsamic vinegar and the bite of mustard, complements the soft, rich meatiness of the shellfish. I prefer Alaskan spotted prawns because they tend to be sweeter and more flavorful than Gulf prawns. Both the prawns and the aïoli can be made ahead.

The salmon entree uses chanterelle mushrooms to add texture and a nutty flavor to a slightly sweet, creamy sauce. Chanterelles are one of the most popular (and most widely available) of the wild local mushrooms because of their rich flavor. When shopping, look for mushrooms that appear fresh—not shriveled and wilted—and free of pine needles and dirt.

At this time of year, king salmon is available in local markets. Although you can buy different species of pen-reared fresh salmon year-round, I prefer the taste of wild-caught fish. Wild rice and a late summer squash would be nice accompaniments to this entree.

For dessert, I have chosen a recipe that requires fresh strawberries. This probably sounds a bit contradictory to my approach of eating food in season. However, there is actually a type of strawberry that produces twice a year, in June and September. If fresh strawberries are unavailable in your area, substitute fresh melon and orange segments, or any other local berries that may still be available. To ease dinner preparations, make the pastry puffs earlier in the day. This dessert is a decorative and celebratory way to round out any evening with friends or family.

Chilled Prawns with Balsamic Mustard Aïoli

Prawns

24 medium Alaskan spotted prawns, peeled and deveined
1 cup white wine
1 cup water
½ onion, coarsely chopped
1 bay leaf
2 garlic cloves, chopped

Aïoli

¼ cup balsamic vinegar
3 tablespoons whole-grain mustard
2 shallots, finely chopped
4 large garlic cloves, finely chopped
2 egg yolks
1¼ cups vegetable oil
Salt and pepper to taste

Lemon slices and fresh greens for garnish

26

To cook the prawns: Place wine, water, onion, bay leaf, and garlic in a large saucepan and bring to a boil. When the mixture is boiling, add the prawns and cook for 3 to 4 minutes, or until they turn pink. Remove from the liquid and cool in ice.

To make the aïoli: In a medium-size mixing bowl, mix vinegar, mustard, shallots, garlic, and egg yolks. Slowly whisk in oil to emulsify. The mixture should thicken as you add the oil. If the aïoli becomes too thick, thin it with a small amount of water or vinegar. When all the oil has been added, season with salt and pepper. You may also add a bit more garlic if you prefer the aïoli stronger. Refrigerate.

Arrange the cooled prawns on a large platter around the Balsamic Mustard Aïoli. Garnish with lemon slices and fresh greens.

Serves 6

VARIATIONS: The aïoli can be made with different types of vinegars, such as a sherry or good red wine vinegar, or flavored with fresh herbs. You can also use a food processor (but not a blender) for this recipe. It will keep in the refrigerator up to 2 weeks.

Poached Salmon with
Chanterelle Cream Sauce

Sauce

¾ cup white wine

½ cup dry sherry

2 shallots, finely chopped

2 garlic cloves, finely chopped

1 cup Fish Stock (see page 226)

½ pound fresh chanterelle mushrooms, cleaned and sliced

½ pint heavy cream

Salt and pepper to taste

¼ pound cleaned whole chanterelle mushrooms for garnish

1 tablespoon butter

Salmon

6 6-ounce salmon fillets

1 cup white wine

1 cup Fish Stock (see page 226)

1 bay leaf

½ teaspoon finely chopped fresh thyme

2 garlic cloves, chopped

2 shallots, chopped

Salt and pepper to taste

To make the sauce and garnish: In a medium-size saucepan, reduce the wine, sherry, shallots, garlic, and Fish Stock until about ⅓ cup of liquid remains. Once reduced, add the sliced mushrooms and cream and reduce until thick. Season with salt and pepper and reserve, keeping warm.

Sauté the whole chanterelles that have been reserved for garnish in butter over high heat, just until tender. Reserve.

To poach the salmon: Preheat oven to 350 degrees. Place salmon fillets in a large, ovenproof sauté pan. Cover the fillets

with wine, stock, bay leaf, thyme, garlic, and shallots. Season
with salt and pepper. Cook over medium heat until liquid
comes to a slow simmer, then move the pan to the oven to
finish cooking, about 5 minutes. Do not overcook the fish.
When done, the flesh should feel firm to the touch, with just a
bit of give.

Remove the fish from the liquid and place on plates.
Sauce and garnish with whole sautéed chanterelles.

Serves 6

29

Strawberry Profiteroles
with Orange Caramel Sauce

Pâte à choux

1 cup water
½ cup unsalted butter
1 tablespoon sugar
½ teaspoon salt
½ teaspoon vanilla
1 cup flour
4 large eggs

Sauce

1 cup sugar
⅓ cup water
1 cup fresh orange juice
1 teaspoon orange zest

2 tablespoons sugar
1 cup whipping cream
1 pint strawberries, cleaned and halved

Fresh mint sprigs for garnish

Preheat oven to 425 degrees.

To make the pâte à choux: In a medium-size saucepan, place water, butter, sugar, salt, and vanilla. Bring to a boil over high heat. When the mixture first comes to a boil, add flour and mix until the dough pulls away from the sides of the pan. Once the dough is completely mixed, cook over low heat, stirring constantly, for 5 minutes to dry the dough. This allows you to add more eggs to the dough, so it will rise better.

When the dough has finished cooking, remove from heat and add the eggs, one at a time, either by hand or using a mixer. Make sure to completely mix each egg in before adding the next one.

Place the dough in a piping bag fitted with a large plain tube and pipe 1½ -inch circular mounds onto a well-greased cookie sheet. Bake about 20 minutes or until golden brown, with a very crispy crust. You do not want the pâte à choux to be soft when removing it from the oven because it will fall and will not hold its shape. Cool and reserve.

To prepare the sauce: Cook sugar and water in a medium-size saucepan over medium heat until golden brown. Do not stir the sugar while caramelizing or the mixture will crystallize. Once the sugar is golden brown, remove from heat and add the orange juice and rind. Stir gently. Return to heat and bring to a boil. Remove from heat and reserve.

To assemble the profiteroles: Add sugar to whipping cream and whip to soft peaks. On 6 small dessert plates, place about ¼ cup of the caramel sauce, saving enough to glaze the tops of the profiteroles.

Cut the pâte à choux pastries in half. Place a bottom half on each plate and fill with strawberries and cream. Replace the tops and drizzle on the remaining sauce. Garnish with fresh mint sprigs.

Serves 6

Duck Consommé with
Celeriac and Sweet Potatoes

Spinach Salad with Pear Thyme Vinaigrette

Baked Lingcod with
Sherry and Shallot Butter Sauce

Pinot Noir Orange Granita

Seared Lamb Loin with
Roasted Garlic Cider Cream

Dark Chocolate Pecan Soufflé
with Spiced Anglaise Sauce

WINE SUGGESTIONS
With the Consommé
Elk Cove Pinot Noir

With the Lingcod
Waterbrook Reserve Chardonnay

With the Lamb
Rex Hill "Willamette Valley" Pinot Noir

BECAUSE IT IS DESIGNED FOR A special occasion, this dinner of many courses is more of a challenge than most of the meals in this book. It can be a feast to honor the arrival of fall and the harvest of all the good things that have been growing during summer, or a Thanksgiving dinner, or a birthday celebration.

The first course is a duck consommé, considered by some people to be difficult to make. However, if you follow directions and make sure the broth does not boil too rapidly while it is clarifying, you will find this soup easy to prepare. It can be made up to a week in advance. I garnish this full-bodied soup with sweet potatoes, for a touch of sweetness, and celeriac, for a crisp celerylike taste.

The soup is followed by spinach salad dressed with a vinaigrette made with fresh pears. The grainy texture of the pear offers a wonderful counterpoint to the smooth texture of the greens. Pears are at their best throughout most of the fall and winter months. Apples may substitute for pears, and the walnuts can be replaced with any other nuts, such as pecans or hazelnuts.

The fish course in this menu is lingcod, which can be found on both coasts. It is a meaty, mild-tasting fish that holds up well with many sauces. Substitute any mild whitefish if you can't find lingcod.

In the transition from fish to lamb, an icy, elegant granita gives you and your guests a pleasant chill. Its name is derived from the word granite, because of the granitelike shape of the ice crystals that form it. The wine and black pepper in this granita cleanse the palate by clearing any fats or strong flavors from your mouth, and help you slide easily into the rich courses ahead.

For the entree, I've chosen lamb loin, although you may use any of your favorite cuts of lamb. Buttery roasted garlic and crisp local apple cider are the stars in the creamy sauce that glosses this lamb. Local, fresh cider that is unfiltered and has no sugar added will produce the best-flavored sauce.

Your fall extravaganza ends on a brave note with a luscious chocolate pecan soufflé. Many people avoid making soufflés because of their notorious reputation for being touchy—they don't rise, they fall when you remove them from the oven, they're too dry, or they're too runny. However, if everything is ready ahead of time, a successful soufflé is merely a matter of timing. If you don't overwhip the egg whites, your soufflé will rise properly. If you don't overmix the whites with the batter, the soufflé won't be runny. (Overmixing at this stage prevents the soufflé from rising at all—instead it will spill all over the bottom of your oven.) If you remember these important points and follow directions carefully, you'll create a dramatic ending to a memorable meal.

Duck Consommé with Celeriac and Sweet Potatoes

½ pound raw duck or chicken meat, chopped or ground finely
1 onion, diced medium
2 leeks, diced medium
2 stalks celery, diced medium
1 carrot, diced medium
1 teaspoon finely chopped fresh thyme
½ teaspoon cracked black pepper
6 egg whites, beaten until frothy
1½ quarts Duck Stock (see page 227)
Salt and pepper to taste
1 celeriac, peeled and medium diced for garnish
1 sweet potato, peeled and diced medium for garnish

In a large bowl, mix together the duck meat, onion, leeks, celery, and carrot. Add thyme, pepper, and egg whites, and incorporate well. Add the vegetable-meat mixture to the Duck Stock in a large, heavy saucepan. Stir well.

Cook the soup over low to medium heat, stirring constantly, until it comes to a boil. Reduce the heat and continue to boil gently for an hour. As the broth cooks, the vegetables, meat, and egg whites form a raft that fortifies and clarifies the consommé. Do not let it boil too fast, or the consommé will become cloudy. Once the soup is finished cooking, carefully strain the clear liquid through a fine sieve lined with cheesecloth. Season with salt and pepper. Reserve, keeping warm until ready to serve (or chill and reheat).

Blanch the diced celeriac and sweet potato quickly in boiling water (about 3 minutes). Cool in ice water and drain. To serve, place garnish in the bottom of warmed bowls and pour hot consommé over the garnish. Serve immediately.

Serves 4

Spinach Salad with Pear Thyme Vinaigrette

Vinaigrette

1 pear, peeled, cored, and diced
½ cup dry white wine
¼ cup rice wine vinegar
3 shallots, finely chopped
2 garlic cloves, finely chopped
2 teaspoons Dijon mustard
¾ cup vegetable oil
1 tablespoon finely chopped fresh thyme
Salt and pepper to taste

Salad

1 bunch spinach, cleaned
1 small head radicchio, cleaned
6 domestic mushrooms, sliced
1 yellow bell pepper, julienned
2 Chinese pear apples or 2 pears, sliced, for garnish

36

To make the vinaigrette: In a small saucepan, cook the diced pear in white wine until tender, then transfer pears and liquid to a blender and puree. Place pear puree, vinegar, shallots, garlic, and mustard in a medium-size bowl and mix well. Slowly whisk in oil to emulsify. Season with fresh thyme, salt, and pepper. Reserve. This dressing will hold up to 2 weeks in the refrigerator. To serve, warm to room temperature and stir again, or heat to make warm spinach salad.

To prepare the salad: Gently tear spinach and radicchio into a large mixing bowl. Add sliced mushrooms, julienned peppers, and ¾ cup of vinaigrette, then toss. Place on plates and garnish with pear apple slices.

Serves 4

Baked Lingcod with
Sherry and Shallot Butter Sauce

Sauce

½ cup dry white wine
½ cup dry sherry
2 garlic cloves, finely chopped
6 shallots, finely chopped
¾ cup unsalted butter
Salt and pepper to taste

Fish

4 4-ounce lingcod fillets
2 tablespoons unsalted butter
½ cup dry white wine
Salt and pepper to taste

Watercress sprigs for garnish

Preheat oven to 350 degrees.

To prepare the sauce: In a heavy, medium-size saucepan over high heat, reduce the white wine, sherry, garlic, and shallots until ¼ cup of liquid remains. Reduce heat to very low and slowly whisk in the butter. Keep the sauce at an even temperature; if it gets too cold or too hot, it will separate. Once the butter is incorporated, season with salt and pepper. Keep the sauce warm—not hot—until serving.

To bake the fish: Place lingcod fillets on a baking sheet, dot with butter, pour white wine over fillets, and season with salt and pepper. Bake for 5 minutes or until slightly firm to the touch. Transfer onto plates, draining the liquid.

Sauce the fish and garnish with watercress sprigs. Serve immediately.

Serves 4

Pinot Noir Orange Granita

1 bottle good-quality pinot noir
½ cup fresh orange juice
¾ cup sugar
2 teaspoons orange zest
1 teaspoon cracked black pepper

Candied Orange Peel (see page 231)
*   and fresh mint leaves for garnish*

Place the first 5 ingredients in a medium-size mixing bowl and stir well until the sugar is dissolved. Place the bowl (uncovered) in the freezer and let the mixture stand until almost frozen. Stir once and return to the freezer until completely frozen. The granita can be made several days ahead. It keeps well in the freezer for several months.

Remove from freezer and stir once more, then serve. Place in chilled wineglasses. Garnish with Candied Orange Peel and fresh mint leaves.

38

Serves 4

VARIATIONS: Granitas can be made with almost any type of wine. Just adjust the sugar according to the sweetness of the wine (the sweeter the wine, the less sugar should be used) so that it has a tart flavor.

Seared Lamb Loin with Roasted Garlic Cider Cream

Cream Sauce

3 shallots, finely chopped
1 apple, diced medium
1 cup apple cider
1 cup white wine
1 pint heavy cream
5 cloves Roasted Garlic (see page 229),
    finely chopped or mashed
Salt and pepper to taste

Lamb

4 5-ounce lamb loins
Salt and pepper to taste
¼ cup vegetable oil

Apple slices and fresh greens for garnish

Preheat oven to 375 degrees.

To make the cream sauce: In a medium-size saucepan, add shallots and diced apple to the apple cider and wine. Cook over high heat until liquid is reduced to ½ cup. Add the heavy cream and reduce again by half or until the mixture is thickened. Pour through a fine strainer and add finely chopped or mashed Roasted Garlic. Season with salt and pepper. Reserve, keeping warm.

To cook the lamb: Remove fat and sliver skin off the lamb loins. Season with salt and pepper. Heat oil in a large ovenproof sauté pan until smoking hot. Sear both sides of the loins and transfer pan to oven. Finish cooking in oven to desired doneness, about 10 minutes for medium rare. Slice lamb, sauce, and garnish.

Serves 4

Dark Chocolate Pecan Soufflé with Spiced Anglaise Sauce

Sauce

2 cups whipping cream

½ cup sugar

4 egg yolks

½ teaspoon each nutmeg, cinnamon, allspice, and ginger

¼ teaspoon ground cloves

¼ cup dark rum

Soufflé

2 tablespoons butter, softened (to coat ramekins)

3 tablespoons sugar (to coat ramekins)

2 ounces bittersweet chocolate

4 egg yolks

½ cup sugar

½ cup unsifted flour

1 cup half-and-half

1 tablespoon cocoa powder

2 tablespoons dark rum

½ cup toasted, chopped pecans

12 egg whites, at room temperature

2 tablespoons plus 2 teaspoons sugar

40

To make the sauce: In a medium-size, heavy saucepan, place cream and ¼ cup of sugar. Bring to a boil. Combine the egg yolks and remaining ¼ cup of sugar. Once combined, warm the yolks slightly by tempering them with a bit of hot cream, then add the yolk mixture slowly into the hot cream.

Cook over low heat, stirring constantly, until the mixture is thick enough to coat the back of a spoon. Remove from heat and mix in the spices and rum. This sauce can be served warm or cold with the soufflé.

To make the soufflé: Preheat oven to 425 degrees. Butter

and sugar 4 6-ounce ramekins or a 1½-quart soufflé dish.

Melt the chocolate in a metal bowl placed over—but not touching—water heated to a rolling boil.

Cream the egg yolks and ½ cup sugar for about 2 minutes, until fluffy and light yellow. Mix in flour and incorporate well.

In a medium-size saucepan, heat the half-and-half just to a boil. Temper the yolks with some of the hot half-and-half, then slowly mix into the rest of the half-and-half. Cook over medium heat, stirring to the consistency of thick soup. Remove from heat and add melted chocolate, cocoa, rum, and pecans. Reserve.

In a clean bowl (preferably copper), whisk egg whites until fluffy, then slowly add remaining sugar and continue whipping until soft peaks form. Do not overwhip the whites or the soufflé won't rise properly.

Place ½ cup of chocolate mixture in a medium-size bowl and gently fold the egg whites into the chocolate. Do not totally blend the egg whites and chocolate: it is better to leave streaks of egg whites to ensure that you do not overmix.

Place batter in prepared soufflé dishes and tap lightly to remove air before putting in the oven. Bake about 15 minutes for individual ramekins; 40 to 50 minutes for a 1½-quart soufflé dish. The soufflé should be browned on top and raised about 1 inch above the top of the dish.

Serve immediately with Spiced Anglaise Sauce.

Serves 4

NOTE: I like the chocolate mixture so much as a dessert sauce that I always make a double batch. The remainder can be frozen to use later. To use as a sauce, thin slightly with milk or half-and-half.

41

PORK TENDERLOIN DINNER FOR 4

Grape Leaves Stuffed with Couscous

Roast Pork Tenderloin
with Braised Leeks and Apples

Orange Cheesecake with Walnut Crust

WINE SUGGESTION
Chateau Ste. Michelle "River Ridge" Chardonnay

IN MAY OF 1988, AT THE INVITATION of the government of Soviet Georgia, I traveled to the Soviet Union with three other cooks from Fullers restaurant and a reporter from the *New York Times*. It was the first time an American group had ever been asked to demonstrate cooking in the Soviet Union. In addition to cooking, we toured the Georgian wine country and were treated to feasts in private homes that lasted for hours. Amid rounds of folk songs and toasts, we sampled over two dozen dishes. The stuffed grape leaves in this menu are my version of an appetizer I enjoyed there. The idea of serving them with fresh yogurt also came from this trip. In the Georgian markets and the wine country, cooks used fresh, tangy yogurts in many ways—including as a dip for stuffed grape leaves.

A savory pork tenderloin, hearty enough for the first chill of fall, but not packed full of heavy cream or butter sauce, is the entree. Pork was once considered to be fatty and unhealthy, but that notion has been proven untrue. The tenderloin—what I use most often—is lean and high in protein. It is best when cooked medium to medium rare. (Unlike the grayed pork chops that we all remember from childhood, pork no longer needs to be cooked to a state of dried, dark jerky to to be considered safe to eat.)

Although braised leeks and apples are a perfect match for pork tenderloin, they also go well with grilled chicken or duck. You can try further variations by substituting ripe pears for apples. If you do, try using a pear wine in the braised mixture to add more pear flavor.

For dessert, a cheesecake enriched by orange zest and Grand Marnier and baked in a spicy walnut crust. This is one of the simplest cheesecake recipes I've ever devised and it can be easily modified—using different nuts in the crust, for example. It always turns out wonderfully.

Grape Leaves Stuffed with Couscous

½ cup couscous
2 cups Chicken Stock (see page 227)
2 shallots, finely chopped
2 garlic cloves, finely chopped
2 large eggs
¼ teaspoon cardamom
Salt and pepper to taste
1 jar prepared grape leaves (about 7 ounces)
1 cup fresh plain yogurt for dipping

Place couscous in a large mixing bowl. Bring 1 cup of the Chicken Stock to a boil with shallots and garlic. Pour the boiling stock over the couscous and allow to stand until the grain has absorbed all the liquid. Let cool. Lightly beat the eggs and add to the couscous along with the cardamom and salt and pepper. Mix well.

Lay the grape leaves flat and place about 2 tablespoons of couscous mixture in the middle of each leaf. Fold the sides in and roll up like an egg roll. Continue until all the filling has been used.

In a large sauté pan, heat the remaining stock to a simmer. Place the grape leaves in the pan one at a time and simmer together gently for about 10 minutes. Remove with a slotted spoon and drain. Serve warm with yogurt on the side.

Makes about 16

VARIATIONS: Try other flavorings in the couscous; for example, add ½ teaspoon cinnamon and ¼ cup currants, or add about ¼ cup of fresh soft goat cheese. Another good variation is to mix in ½ cup Italian pork sausage. If you add sausage, increase the cooking time another 3 to 5 minutes.

The yogurt can also be flavored with mint or parsley.

Roast Pork Tenderloin
with Braised Leeks and Apples

3 leeks, whites only
2 Granny Smith apples, peeled and cored
2 tablespoons unsalted butter
½ cup white wine
½ cup sherry
2 tablespoons vegetable oil
2 large pork tenderloins, all fat removed
1 teaspoon cracked black pepper
Salt to taste

Preheat oven to 350 degrees.

Cut the leeks in half lengthwise and clean well. Julienne the leek halves and reserve. Thinly slice the apples. In a large, ovenproof sauté pan, heat the butter. Add the apples and sauté slightly over high heat. Add the leeks and toss to mix. Add wine and sherry and reserve over low heat.

In a very large, ovenproof sauté pan, heat oil until smoking hot. Season the tenderloins with cracked black pepper. Salt to taste. Place tenderloins in the pan and brown well to sear in all the juices.

Move the pans with braised apples and leeks and the pork tenderloins to the oven for about 10 to 15 minutes to finish cooking. The meat should be medium to medium rare. Remove from the oven and slice the meat on an angle. Season the apples and leeks to taste, transfer to a serving platter, and arrange with sliced meat.

Serves 4

45

Orange Cheesecake with Walnut Crust

Crust
1½ cups finely ground walnuts
½ cup sugar
Pinch each of cinnamon, nutmeg, and allspice
¼ cup butter, melted

Filling
1½ cups sugar
1½ pounds cream cheese, softened
4 large eggs
1 teaspoon orange juice concentrate
1 teaspoon orange zest
¼ cup Grand Marnier

Orange segments and whipped cream for garnish

To make the crust: Place ground nuts, sugar, and spices in a medium-size mixing bowl. Mix thoroughly. Drizzle in butter and mix again. If the mixture is too dry and crumbly, add another tablespoon of melted butter. Press evenly on bottom of a lightly greased 9-inch springform pan. Chill for 30 minutes.

Preheat oven to 350 degrees.

To make the filling: Cream the sugar and cream cheese together with a mixer on medium speed. Slowly add each egg, mixing well after each one. Add the orange juice concentrate, zest, and Grand Marnier. Blend thoroughly and pour into the prepared pan. Bake about 1 hour, or until a knife inserted comes out clean.

Cool completely before removing sides of springform pan. Serve with fresh orange segments and whipped cream.

Makes 1 9-inch cheesecake

CRAB SANDWICH AND SALAD LUNCH
FOR 6

Crab Club Sandwich on Roasted Shallot Brioche

Grilled Eggplant Salad

Pecan Tart with Brandy Custard

WITH THIS LUNCHEON YOU NEED to spend some time in the kitchen the day before: once your company arrives, they will marvel at the ease with which lunch is served. Your first and most ambitious task is to bake the bread. Brioche is a butter- and egg-rich bread, which means if you're counting calories, count this sandwich out. The whole thing tops in at about 1,200 calories, but the flavors and texture of the bread are worth the extra calories. A bit of sugar and oven-roasted shallots give this bread a sweet flavor with a lot of depth.

The crab in this sandwich is mixed with Basil Thyme Mayonnaise, then layered with tomato slices and lettuce. When you buy the crab, I suggest you stick to already cracked crabmeat. (The time it takes to pick crabmeat from whole crabs isn't worth the small saving of money per pound.)

The eggplant salad can be grilled and layered the day before, refrigerated, then allowed to come to room temperature. When selecting eggplants at the market, look for the darkest ones, free of blemishes or soft spots. For this or any vinaigrette calling for olive oil, use extra virgin—it is the best quality oil you can buy for salad dressings. Extra virgin is the oil that comes from the first press, so it is not bitter, and the flavors are much cleaner and more defined than in virgin olive oil.

A creamy pecan tart is a smooth ending to this fall lunch. The mascarpone (a soft Italian cream cheese) adds richness to the custard and goes nicely with the hearty pecan. Hazelnuts work well also. The tart can be baked ahead, unless you plan to serve it warm. In that case, time it so the tart comes out of the oven just as sandwiches are being served. This way it will be cool enough to cut, but still warm.

Crab Club Sandwich on Roasted Shallot Brioche

Basil Thyme Mayonnaise

¼ cup white wine vinegar
2 shallots, finely chopped
2 garlic cloves, finely chopped
2 tablespoons Dijon mustard
2 egg yolks
1½ cups vegetable oil
1 teaspoon finely chopped fresh basil
1 teaspoon finely chopped fresh thyme
Salt and pepper to taste

Crab Mixture

2 cups fresh Dungeness crabmeat
¾ cup Basil Thyme Mayonnaise

1 loaf Roasted Shallot Brioche (recipe follows)
2 medium tomatoes, sliced
1 head red leaf or other seasonal lettuce, cleaned
1 bunch chives, cut into 1-inch lengths
1 red bell pepper, julienned

49

To make the mayonnaise: In a mixer or a food processor fitted with a metal blade, place vinegar, shallots, garlic, mustard, and egg yolks. With motor running, slowly drizzle in oil. Process to emulsify and thicken. Add herbs and seasonings and process to mix. Refrigerate until needed.

To assemble the open-faced sandwiches: Mix crabmeat with ½ cup of Basil Thyme Mayonnaise. Spread remaining ¼ cup of mayonnaise on toasted bread slices (12 slices). Layer toast with lettuce leaves, a tomato slice, and crab mixture. Garnish the top with chive strips and julienned red pepper.

Serves 6 (2 slices per person)

Roasted Shallot Brioche

¼ cup sugar

1 teaspoon salt

2 packages dry yeast

4½ cups flour

1 cup milk

1 cup butter

5 eggs

6 Oven Roasted Shallots (see page 229), chopped

1 egg

2 teaspoons water

In a very large bowl, combine sugar, salt, yeast, and 1½ cups flour. In a medium-size saucepan, heat milk and butter until very hot, about 120 degrees. With a mixer on low speed, gradually beat liquid into dry ingredients. Beat about 2 minutes, scraping the bowl. Mix in eggs, then add remaining flour 1 cup at a time to make a soft dough. Add chopped shallots and beat for 5 minutes.

Place dough in a greased bowl and cover. Let rise for 1 hour or until doubled. Punch down dough, grease, cover, and let sit overnight in the refrigerator. The next day punch down dough again and allow to rest 15 minutes. Divide the dough in half. Shape both halves into loaves and place in greased and floured 9-inch-by-5-inch loaf pans. Cover and allow to rise until double in size, about 1 hour.

Preheat oven to 350 degrees.

Brush raised loaves with 1 egg beaten with 2 teaspoons of water. Bake about 1 hour. Cool before slicing.

Makes 2 loaves

HINT: Freeze the second loaf to use later for more club sandwiches or a variety of other sandwiches.

Grilled Eggplant Salad

Balsamic Vinaigrette
2 tablespoons balsamic vinegar
2 shallots, finely chopped
3 garlic cloves, finely chopped
1 tablespoon Dijon mustard
⅓ cup extra virgin olive oil
½ teaspoon cracked black pepper
Salt to taste

2 medium eggplants, sliced about ¼ inch thick
2 tablespoons olive oil
Salt and pepper to taste

To make vinaigrette: Place vinegar, shallots, garlic, and mustard in a bowl and mix together. Slowly whisk in oil to emulsify. Season with cracked pepper and salt. Reserve.

To make the salad: Brush eggplant with olive oil and cook on a hot, greased grill on both sides. Once eggplant slices have been grilled, lay them on a platter and pour vinaigrette over them. Serve at room temperature.

Serves 6

51

Pecan Tart with Brandy Custard

Crust

2 cups flour
½ cup brown sugar
½ teaspoon vanilla
Pinch salt
1 cup unsalted butter

Filling

1 cup half-and-half
½ cup mascarpone
½ cup sugar
3 eggs
½ teaspoon cinnamon
2 tablespoons brandy

2 cups toasted, coarsely chopped pecans

Preheat oven to 350 degrees.

To make the crust: Place flour, brown sugar, vanilla, and salt in food processor fitted with a metal blade. While the machine is running, slowly add butter. Allow machine to process until dough forms a ball. Remove dough from bowl of food processor and press onto bottom and sides of a greased, 12-inch tart pan. Bake for 10 minutes. Remove and cool.

To make the filling: In a medium-size mixing bowl, blend half-and-half with the mascarpone. Add sugar and eggs and mix well. Stir in cinnamon and brandy.

To assemble: Spread chopped pecans in the tart crust. Pour filling over the pecans. Bake (at 350 degrees) until custard is set, about 30 to 40 minutes or until a knife inserted comes out clean. Serve warm or cool.

Makes 1 12-inch tart

Indian Summer Duck Luncheon
for 6

Oysters Baked on the Half Shell
with Hazelnut Lemon Butter

Sliced Duck Breast over Julienned Vegetables
with Orange Walnut Vinaigrette

Pear and Fig Compote

Wine Suggestion
Snoqualmie Reserve Merlot

Plan this lunch for those late days of Indian summer, when the air is crisp but the sun still warm enough for a leisurely meal on the deck. Dining outdoors—what Italians call al fresco—demands that you spend as little time in the kitchen as possible. That's why, as in many of the menus in this book, you can prepare everything ahead of time.

Baked oysters topped with a dollop of savory hazelnut butter are a delicious opener for this meal. Oysters are plump and at their peak of flavor in the fall. There are several varieties grown in Puget Sound waters, including the tiny Olympia oyster, which is considered a local delicacy. I recommend the larger Pacific or European varieties for this appetizer, however, since the little Olympia is best eaten raw.

When shucking an oyster, place it on a towel or use a mitt to protect your hand from both the raspy shell and the potential slip of a knife. Insert the shucking knife along the edge of the shell, slice the adductor muscle inside, and twist the flat of the shell to pry it off. It's important to slice the muscle so that the meat doesn't tear when you pull the top shell off. If you want to shuck the oysters before your guests arrive—or have someone at the seafood market do it for you—keep them moist in the refrigerator by covering them with wet paper towels and plastic wrap. If you don't open the oysters until you are ready to use them, they will keep in the shell for several days in the refrigerator.

Using flavored butters, such as the Hazelnut Lemon Butter, is a simple and flexible way to dress up shellfish, as well as grilled fish, chicken, or vegetables. Such butters keep in the freezer for several months, so you can even make several varieties at a time. Store them in jars or roll them into logs, wrap them in plastic wrap, and slice off just the amount you need.

The entree for this meal can also be prepared ahead of

time. Buy whole ducks for this dish; after you bone the breasts for lunch, you can use the legs and carcass to make Duck Stock (page 227). In this recipe the dark, rich duck meat contrasts nicely with the crisp, tangy julienned vegetables in vinaigrette. If you prefer a milder or less fatty meat, substitute chicken or turkey breast. You can also vary this recipe by trying different vegetables or changing the flavors in the vinaigrette.

One of my favorite ways to serve fruit during the fall and winter is in a warm compote. The fruit can be prepared and cooked at the last minute. Serve the compote alone, or poured over pound cake or puff pastry squares. It is especially good topped with a scoop of ice cream.

Oysters Baked on the Half Shell with Hazelnut Lemon Butter

Butter

½ cup toasted hazelnuts
3 shallots, chopped
4 garlic cloves, chopped
1 cup unsalted butter, softened
Juice of 1 lemon
2 teaspoons lemon zest
¼ cup dry white wine or sherry
Salt and pepper to taste

24 to 30 fresh oysters, shucked on the half shell

Seaweed or rock salt and lemon twists for garnish

Preheat oven to 350 degrees.

To make the butter: In a food processor, grind the toasted hazelnuts, chopped shallots, and garlic to a fine consistency. Add the softened butter and run the machine long enough to fully incorporate it. Add lemon juice, zest, wine, salt, and pepper. Process again until the liquid is mixed in. Store in a jar or shape into a roll and wrap tightly with plastic wrap until ready to use. The butter can be kept refrigerated for several weeks or frozen up to several months.

To bake the oysters: Place the fresh oysters on their half shells on a bed of rock salt on a cookie sheet. Top each one with a tablespoon of butter. Bake for 5 minutes or until they plump.

Serve warm on a bed of seaweed or rock salt garnished with lemon twists.

Serves 6 (4 to 5 oysters per person)

Sliced Duck Breast over Julienned Vegetables with Orange Walnut Vinaigrette

Vinaigrette

½ cup orange juice

¼ cup white wine vinegar

2 shallots, finely chopped

2 garlic cloves, finely chopped

1 tablespoon Dijon mustard

2 teaspoons orange zest

½ cup vegetable oil

¼ cup walnut oil

Salt and pepper to taste

Vegetables

1 red pepper, julienned

1 zucchini, julienned

1 yellow squash, julienned

2 carrots, julienned

¼ pound snow peas, julienned

½ bulb fennel, julienned

3 whole duck breasts, boned

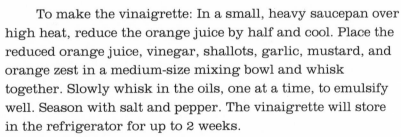

To make the vinaigrette: In a small, heavy saucepan over high heat, reduce the orange juice by half and cool. Place the reduced orange juice, vinegar, shallots, garlic, mustard, and orange zest in a medium-size mixing bowl and whisk together. Slowly whisk in the oils, one at a time, to emulsify well. Season with salt and pepper. The vinaigrette will store in the refrigerator for up to 2 weeks.

Toss the julienned vegetables together in a large mixing bowl and set aside.

Preheat oven to 375 degrees.

To prepare the duck breasts: Heat a large, ovenproof

sauté pan over high heat until very hot. Brown the duck breast, skin side down. (Do not add any oil to the pan; the duck will brown in its own fat.) Transfer the pan to the oven. Continue to cook it skin side down the majority of the time to cook off most of the fat. I suggest a medium doneness for best results. Depending on the size of the breasts, this should take 10 to 12 minutes. When the duck is done, take it out of the oven, remove from the pan, and set aside to cool.

To assemble: Toss the vegetables with the vinaigrette (reserve a small amount) and distribute evenly on each plate. Slice the cooled duck breasts and arrange on top of the vegetables. Drizzle the reserved vinaigrette over the duck slices and serve immediately.

Serves 6

VARIATIONS: You may change the flavor of this dressing by adding fresh herbs or other flavored oils. Two combinations I like are sesame oil with cilantro and hazelnut oil with thyme.

58

Different vegetables may be used in this dish, including celeriac, red or Walla Walla onions, or scallions.

Pear and Fig Compote

¼ cup unsalted butter
5 pears, peeled, cored, and thinly sliced
4 fresh figs, quartered
⅓ cup port
¼ cup Simple Syrup (see page 230)
1 cinnamon stick

French vanilla ice cream (optional)

In a large sauté pan over high heat, melt the butter, then lightly sauté the pears and figs. Pour in port and reduce slightly. Add syrup and cinnamon stick and cook over medium heat until the pears are tender, about 5 minutes. Remove the cinnamon stick and spoon onto plates.

Serve the compote warm, either alone or with a scoop of French vanilla ice cream on top.

Serves 6

59

VARIATIONS: This warm compote can be made with just about any fruit. I often make it with fresh berries and try different liqueurs, such as Amaretto or Grand Marnier.

BREAKFAST OF BAKED EGGS AND ROSEMARY POTATOES FOR 4

Black Muscat Poached Pears with Crème Fraîche

Rosemary Cottage Potatoes

Baked Eggs with Tarragon and Smoked Salmon

WHILE OUT OF THE ORDINARY, this delicious breakfast is really very simple and—like many of my meals—much of it can be prepared ahead of time. The poached pears, for example, are tastier if made the day before. Sitting in the poaching liquid, they will turn a beautiful ruby red on the outside, fading to white on the inside. The color makes a striking display when you slice and fan the pears on a plate. Make sure the pears are not too ripe, or they will turn to mush when sliced.

The breakfast potatoes, too, can be done ahead (about a half hour) and kept warm; but don't hold them too long because they tend to dry out. If you are not a fan of rosemary, other stronger herbs, such as savory and oregano, work well. The pan should be very hot when cooking so that the potatoes will be crisp on the outside and soft on the inside. Use virgin—not extra virgin—olive oil. While the extra virgin is preferred for salad dressings, it burns easily and should not be used for frying.

An old childhood favorite of mine—baked eggs—accompanies the crunchy potatoes. I've just recently started making them again. Until now, the last time I made any type of baked egg dish was in the early morning pantry class at the Culinary Institute of America. These eggs are easy and tasty to make, but don't get hooked on them because they are loaded with cholesterol. Once you have assembled the eggs, the only last-minute things to do are baking and garnishing.

Baked eggs are easy to vary. You can add sautéed mushrooms or different cheeses, such as a good-quality Parmesan. Experiment with different layers and combinations of cheeses, herbs, and smoked meats and fish. Some great combinations are spinach, mushrooms, and aged cheddar; or fresh tomatoes, basil leaves, and Parmesan.

Black Muscat Poached Pears with Crème Fraîche

1 bottle good-quality black muscat wine
½ cup sugar
½ teaspoon orange zest
1 cinnamon stick
4 pears, peeled and cored
1 cup Crème Fraîche (see page 230)

In a large saucepan, heat wine, sugar, orange zest, and cinnamon stick over high heat until boiling. Place pears in the liquid and lower heat. Simmer the pears until tender when pricked with a fork. Remove from heat and refrigerate in poaching liquid until serving (preferably overnight).

Remove pears from liquid with a slotted spoon. Slice and fan on a plate or cut into halves. Serve with Crème Fraîche, on the side or drizzled over the pears.

Serves 4

Rosemary Cottage Potatoes

2 tablespoons olive oil
6 medium red or new potatoes, washed and cut into thin
*   wedges (about 8 wedges per potato)*
½ teaspoon finely chopped fresh rosemary
1 teaspoon cracked black pepper
Salt to taste

Heat olive oil in a large sauté pan until smoking hot. Add potatoes and cook over high heat until they start to brown. Turn to brown the other side.

Once the potatoes are completely browned, season with rosemary, pepper, and salt. Drain onto a paper towel and serve hot.

Serves 4

Baked Eggs with Tarragon and Smoked Salmon

1 tablespoon unsalted butter, softened
¼ pound cold-smoked salmon (lox)
1 teaspoon finely chopped fresh tarragon
½ cup grated Yakima Gouda cheese
8 eggs
Salt and pepper to taste
Pinch of cayenne

Fresh tarragon sprigs for garnish

Preheat oven to 325 degrees.

Butter 4 6-ounce, ovenproof ramekins. Place about 1 ounce of smoked salmon on the bottom of each ramekin, followed by tarragon and cheese. On top of the cheese, crack 2 eggs per cup, and season with salt, pepper, and cayenne.

Bake just until whites set, about 15 to 20 minutes. Remove from the oven and garnish with fresh tarragon sprigs. Serve hot.

Serves 4

Ginger Waffles with Pumpkin Butter

Grilled Pineapple

O<small>N</small> S<small>UNDAY MORNINGS WHEN MY</small> family and I are going to bundle up and venture outside for the day, this is the breakfast of choice. Most people use pre-made waffle mixes because they feel they are too busy to take the time to make anything from scratch. With a full-time career and a three-year-old son, I, too, am one of those busy people. But I do take time to make these Ginger Waffles, which taste so unique they're worth the extra effort. They are also surprisingly quick and easy to make.

The accompanying Pumpkin Butter—on the other hand—is easy, but takes a bit of time and planning. If you are too pressed to make Pumpkin Butter, make the waffles anyway. They taste great with a good-quality, store-bought raspberry jam. I love the way the ginger marries with the sweet tang of raspberries. What you won't get buying a jar of jam, however, is the aroma of spices and pumpkin filling your home and the cozy memories of your grandmother's house or Thanksgiving dinners it will stir.

Pumpkin Butter is one of the few things I have time to make in the fall to give away at Christmas—that should give some indication of how easy it is. There is some dirty work, peeling and cleaning the pumpkin of seeds. Once this is done, however, there is little else to do except to cook it, puree, and reduce the pulp. (I use a hand-held mixer to puree it; it's less messy and you don't need to transfer the hot pumpkin back and forth between blender and pot.)

A breakfast of waffles as special as these needs no more than a simple accompaniment—Grilled Pineapple, with a classic touch of butter and rum. Served with fresh fruit sorbet, this pineapple also makes a wonderful dessert.

Ginger Waffles with Pumpkin Butter

2 cups milk
1 teaspoon finely chopped gingerroot
1¾ cups flour
1 teaspoon baking soda
1 teaspoon baking powder
½ teaspoon salt
1 teaspoon ground ginger
⅓ cup vegetable oil
2 large eggs
Pumpkin Butter (recipe follows)
Sour cream

Place milk and fresh chopped ginger in a saucepan. Slowly bring to a boil over high heat. Continue cooking for just a couple of minutes, then strain ginger from the milk. Reserve milk and cool to room temperature.

Grease and heat the waffle iron.

In a large bowl, place all dry ingredients and mix well. Add cooled milk and eggs. Mix until well blended.

Pour batter into the hot, greased waffle iron. Cook waffles about 3 to 5 minutes or until waffle iron starts to emit steam.

Dust waffles with powdered sugar and serve warm, topped with Pumpkin Butter and sour cream.

Serves 4

67

Pumpkin Butter

2 2½-pound pumpkins
2 cups apple cider
1 cup brown sugar
1 teaspoon cinnamon
½ teaspoon allspice
½ teaspoon ground cloves
½ teaspoon nutmeg

Peel pumpkins and remove seeds. Cut pumpkins into large chunks and place in a large saucepan with the apple cider. Cook over medium heat until the pumpkin chunks are tender.

Using a hand-held mixer, puree pumpkin and cider (or transfer to a blender or food processor, puree, then return to saucepan). Add sugar and spices. Cook until the mixture is very thick, about the consistency of applesauce.

Cool and store in the refrigerator in a covered jar. This butter will keep up to 1 month.

Makes 1½ quarts

Grilled Pineapple

1 medium-size ripe pineapple, peeled and cored
¼ cup brown sugar
1 tablespoon unsalted butter, softened
¼ cup dark rum

Slice the pineapple into ¼-inch-thick rounds. In a small bowl, blend together sugar and softened butter, then mix in rum. Spray grill with nonstick spray or grease well, and preheat over medium to high heat. Coat each of the pineapple rounds in sugar mixture and quickly grill each side until golden. Place on a serving dish and serve hot or cold.

Serves 4

WINTER

NEW YEAR'S EVE DINNER for 6

Oysters on the Half Shell
with Pinot Noir Mignonette

Sautéed Prawns with Daikon and Sweet Peppers

Phyllo Cups with Marinated Pears and Oranges
on Champagne Sabayon

WINE SUGGESTION
Mount Baker Gewürztraminer

WORKING IN A RESTAURANT, I rarely have a New Year's Eve off. When I do, I prefer to ring in the New Year with champagne and an elegant dinner at home with friends, rather than celebrate in a crowded bar or restaurant. This menu does not require much preparation beforehand—if your life is anything like mine around the holidays, who has time to cook?

Oysters served raw on the half shell should be the freshest ones you can find. If you are lucky enough to live close to the ocean, that means local oysters. Today, the varieties of the principal species grown in Puget Sound—Pacific, European or Belon, and Olympia oysters—generally refer to a particular growing area or grower, Shoalwater Bay, Westcott Bay, and Hamma Hamma to name a few. Each has a distinct flavor that is the result of growing conditions such as water temperature and salinity. To ensure their freshness, don't open the oysters too far ahead of dinner and keep them icy cold once opened.

The mignonette is a sauce with a base of wine and vinegar that is often served with oysters. This one is made from pinot noir and red wine vinegar, spiced with cracked black pepper and shallots to complement the clean ocean flavor of the oysters. It can be made up to two weeks ahead of time and kept in the refrigerator.

For the main dish, I use large prawns (16 to 20 per pound). If you clean and devein the prawns and cut all the vegetables beforehand, you can finish preparing this dish at the last minute. The sweet flavor of the prawns and the bell peppers is a nice combination, and the daikon adds a spicy dimension, but you may want to substitute your own vegetable choices.

Phyllo dough is one of my favorite pastries to work with because it is so versatile. It changes with each filling or dish. I've tried it with everything from singing scallops to raspberry mousse. It also makes an easy spring and summer base for fresh berries, topped with a bit of brown sugar and Crème Frâiche. In this recipe, phyllo forms a cup that is filled with spicy marinated pears and oranges on a creamy champagne sabayon, a foamy, custardlike dessert sauce. Although you can prepare them ahead, I suggest that you do not make the cups too far in advance, because they can become stale.

Oysters on the Half Shell with Pinot Noir Mignonette

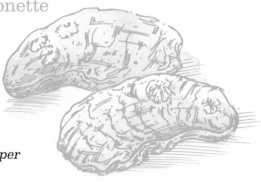

Mignonette

1 cup pinot noir
½ cup red wine vinegar
3 shallots, finely chopped
2 garlic cloves, finely chopped
2 tablespoons honey
1 tablespoon cracked black pepper

2 to 3 dozen fresh oysters, cleaned and shucked
    on the half shell
Cracked ice or rock salt
Seaweed for garnish

Place pinot noir, red wine vinegar, shallots, garlic, honey, and cracked pepper in a medium-size saucepan. Bring to a boil over medium to high heat. Remove and cool. If you are not going to use the mignonette right away, store it in an airtight container in your refrigerator. It will keep up to 2 weeks.

Arrange the oysters on a tray covered with ice or rock salt and decorated with seaweed. Stir the mignonette well. Spoon a small amount over each oyster to coat. Serve immediately.

Serves 6

NOTE: If you use Olympia oysters, you may wish to serve more per person since they are much smaller than other species.

Sautéed Prawns with Daikon and Sweet Peppers

2 tablespoons unsalted butter
3 garlic cloves, finely chopped
2 shallots, finely chopped
2 tablespoons finely chopped gingerroot
36 large prawns, peeled and deveined
1 large daikon, julienned
2 red bell peppers, julienned
1 yellow bell pepper, julienned
2 tablespoons sesame oil
Salt and pepper to taste84
Basmati rice flavored with lemon grass,
     or Chinese noodles (optional)
Fresh cilantro and pickled ginger for garnish

Heat the butter in a large sauté pan over high heat until it starts to bubble. Lightly sauté garlic, shallots, and ginger. Add prawns and cook just until they turn pink. Add julienned daikon and sweet peppers and sauté another 2 to 3 minutes. Add sesame oil and season with salt and pepper.

Remove from heat and serve over rice or with Chinese noodles. Garnish with fresh cilantro and pickled ginger.

Serves 6

VARIATIONS AND SUBSTITUTIONS: If you don't care for shrimp, make this dish with scallops or crabmeat instead. You can also substitute other fresh vegetables for the ones given in the recipe. Snow peas, bok choy, or carrots would all work nicely. Sliced shiitake mushrooms are another interesting addition.

Phyllo Cups with Marinated Pears and Oranges on Champagne Sabayon

Phyllo Cups
½ box of phyllo dough sheets cut into quarters
2 tablespoons butter, melted
¼ cup sugar

Poached Pears
3 pears, peeled and cored
2 cups dry white wine
½ cup sugar
1 cinnamon stick

Marinated Oranges and Pears
3 oranges, peeled and segmented
3 poached pears, thinly sliced
¼ cup Grand Marnier
2 tablespoons sugar
Pinch of cinnamon
Pinch of nutmeg
¼ teaspoon vanilla

Sabayon
1 cup champagne
½ cup sugar
5 egg yolks
1 cup whipping cream, whipped

Fresh mint for garnish

Preheat oven to 350 degrees.

To prepare the phyllo cups: Grease a muffin pan and line the inside of each cup with 2 sheets of the quartered phyllo dough. Lightly butter and sugar the top layer, then repeat with another 2 more sheets of phyllo. Bake until golden brown, about 5 to 10 minutes. Reserve.

To poach the pears: Place pears in a large saucepan. Add white wine, sugar, and cinnamon stick and cook over medium heat until tender (not mushy). Remove from liquid, cool, and slice.

To marinate the oranges and pears: Place fruit in a medium-size mixing bowl. Add Grand Marnier, sugar, cinnamon, nutmeg, and vanilla. Marinate at least 2 hours.

To make the sabayon: Place champagne, sugar, and egg yolks in a metal bowl and mix well. Set the bowl over a water bath on high heat (the bowl should not touch the water). Whisk continuously, cooking until the mixture thickens to the consistency of soft whipped cream. Cool slightly and fold in whipped cream.

To assemble: Place the phyllo cups on individual plates and fill with marinated fruit. Pour sabayon sauce over half the cup and onto the plate. Garnish with fresh mint.

Serves 6

GLAZED PORK TENDERLOIN FOR 4

Scallop Ceviche

Seasonal Greens with
Oregon Blue Cheese Dressing

Roasted Pork Tenderloin with Raisin Glacé

Chocolate Hazelnut Torte

WINE SUGGESTION
Columbia "Red Willow" Cabernet Sauvignon

Winters in Seattle are usually very mild, with rare snows, but plenty of rain. This is when I most enjoy spending time by the fireplace with a good book and a snifter of fine brandy. I also like to entertain in the winter, because nothing brightens a cold, gray day more than a warm, satisfying meal shared with friends.

The first course is a scallop ceviche, a dish often found in Latin cooking. I use it on a winter menu because its flavors stir memories of tropical places and sunshine, and because it uses citrus juice, which is always available in winter. (Oranges, lemons, and limes are best during winter.) Ceviche is fish that is "cooked" by acids in the lime and orange juices and rice wine vinegar (lemon and grapefruit juice could also be used). Since you do not heat the scallops, buy the freshest ones you can find. Also, a light whitefish can be used instead of scallops. In order to give the flavors time to blend well, this appetizer should be made the day before serving.

The salad is dressed with a Northwest blue cheese that is mild and creamy, which is more appealing to many people than a drier, stronger blue cheese. Cucumbers, tomatoes, mushrooms, and red leaf lettuce are tossed with the blue cheese dressing and placed on a colorful bed of butter lettuce and radicchio. Feel free to garnish this salad with any seasonal vegetables you like.

Oddly, this menu's entree couples one of my favorite meats with one of my least favorite foods—raisins. Why do I use them here? I like the sweetness they add to the Veal Stock. I strain the raisins out before serving the sauce, but if you are a raisin lover, leave them in. Pork tenderloin is a versatile meat, delicate enough to go with just about any sauce and inexpensive. I serve tenderloin frequently at home, and it is a regular menu item at Fullers.

Make the chocolate torte the day before your dinner, but hold the powdered sugar until just before serving. If you're a devoted chocoholic and you want to make the torte even richer than it already is, glaze it with 4 ounces of semisweet chocolate, 2 tablespoons butter, and 2 tablespoons heavy cream melted together over a boiling water bath. Let the chocolate mixture cook to thicken, pour it over the cooled torte, and refrigerate until cool. To make the torte easier to cut, remove it from the refrigerator 20 minutes before serving. This will warm it just enough so the chocolate glaze won't crack and you'll have a bakery-perfect torte.

Scallop Ceviche

1 pound sea scallops
1 red bell pepper, julienned
1 yellow bell pepper, julienned
1 leek, white part only, julienned
1 orange, peeled and segmented
1 lime, peeled and segmented
Juice of 1 lime
Juice of 1 orange
2 shallots, finely chopped
2 garlic cloves, finely chopped
¼ cup rice wine vinegar
½ cup vegetable oil
Salt and pepper to taste

Curly endive or greens for garnish

Place scallops, peppers, leek, and fruit segments in a medium-size mixing bowl and toss together. Mix lime juice, orange juice, shallots, garlic, and vinegar in a small bowl. Whisk in oil and season with salt and pepper (this dressing will not emulsify).

Pour dressing over the scallops and vegetables and refrigerate in a covered bowl for 6 hours. To serve, arrange on plates and garnish with curly endive or other greens.

Serves 4

VARIATIONS: This preparation works well with any mild whitefish, such as halibut or cod. The juice from half a grapefruit is a nice addition to the recipe.

Seasonal Greens
with Oregon Blue Cheese Dressing

Dressing
¼ cup white wine vinegar
2 tablespoons Dijon mustard
2 egg yolks
2 shallots, finely chopped
2 garlic cloves, finely chopped
1¼ cups vegetable oil
4 ounces Oregon blue cheese, crumbled
2 tablespoons sour cream
Salt and pepper to taste

Salad
1 head butter lettuce, rinsed
1 small head radicchio, rinsed
1 head red leaf lettuce, rinsed
1 cucumber, peeled and seeded
4 Roma tomatoes, quartered
5 large mushroom caps, sliced

83

To make the dressing: In a medium-size mixing bowl, mix together vinegar, mustard, egg yolks, shallots, and garlic. Slowly add vegetable oil, whisking to emulsify. Once all the oil is added, stir in the blue cheese and sour cream. Season with salt and pepper. This dressing stores up to 2 weeks in the refrigerator.

To assemble the salad: Line each salad plate with alternating leaves of butter lettuce and radicchio. Tear the red leaf lettuce into a medium-size mixing bowl. Add the vegetables and about ¼ cup of dressing and toss. Distribute salad onto the prepared salad plates and serve immediately.

Serves 4

Roasted Pork Tenderloin with Raisin Glacé

3 shallots, finely chopped
2 garlic cloves, finely chopped
1 cup dry, hearty red wine
1 quart Veal Stock (see page 228)
½ cup raisins
About ¼ cup leftover mushroom scraps (i.e., peels and stems)
Salt and pepper to taste

2 tablespoons vegetable oil
3 medium pork tenderloins
Salt and pepper to taste

Golden raisins and watercress for garnish

Preheat oven to 350 degrees.

Place shallots, garlic, and wine in a large saucepan and reduce liquid over high heat until ¼ cup remains. Add Veal Stock, raisins, and mushroom scraps. Reduce by half, or until the sauce is thick and flavorful. Season to taste. Strain sauce and reserve, keeping warm.

Heat oil in a large, ovenproof sauté pan until smoking hot. Trim fat from pork and season with salt and pepper. Sear the tenderloins until evenly brown. Transfer pan to oven to finish cooking, about 7 minutes for medium to medium rare. Remove tenderloin from pan and slice at an angle. Distribute onto 4 warmed plates. Sauce and garnish with golden raisins and watercress.

Serves 4

Chocolate Hazelnut Torte

½ pound bittersweet chocolate
½ pound unsalted butter
¾ cup sugar
¾ cup dark cocoa powder, sifted
6 eggs, slightly beaten
2 cups ground toasted hazelnuts
¼ cup Frangelico hazelnut liqueur
Pinch of cinnamon

Powdered sugar for dusting
Fresh mint sprigs for garnish

Preheat oven to 350 degrees. Fill a heavy roasting pan with about ¼ inch of warm water and place in oven.

In a medium-size metal bowl set over a pan of boiling water, melt the bittersweet chocolate and butter. Remove from heat and mix in sugar and cocoa powder. Fold in the slightly beaten eggs (do not overmix when adding the eggs). Stir in hazelnuts, liqueur, and cinnamon.

Pour the mixture into a greased and floured 9-inch cake pan. Set in the water bath and bake for 40 minutes, or until a knife inserted comes out clean. Cool for 5 minutes before turning onto a plate, then cool completely. Dust well with powdered sugar and garnish with mint sprigs.

Makes 1 9-inch torte

85

Après-Ski Dinner for 6

Warm Spinach Salad with Honey Dijon Dressing

Northwest Seafood Stew

The Ultimate Brownie

Wine Suggestion
Ridge Merlot

THE NORTHWEST IS BLESSED WITH some of the most beautiful mountains in North America. From Seattle, where I live, the Cascade Range rises to the east and the Olympics dominate the horizon to the west. Spending a day in the mountains skiing or playing in the snow is a favorite pastime among my friends and family. On such a day, food is the first thing we all think about when we head home.

This dinner was designed for just such a day. It is warm, quick, and fulfilling. Everything can be prepared ahead of time so your cold and ravenous friends don't have to wait. The spinach salad can be prepped ahead of time: make the dressing and clean and tear the spinach. The salad then can be easily put together at the last moment before serving to hungry fans. If you want to add to the texture of the salad, throw in some curly endive and radicchio.

For the entree, make the soup base days ahead of serving and freeze it. Move it to the refrigerator the day before to let it thaw overnight. All you need to do at dinnertime is cook the fish and add it to the base to make a hearty and warm main course. Be sure to use only the freshest fish when making the stew, and don't buy it more than a day ahead of time.

Of course, people who've had their appetites whetted by mountain air deserve a satisfying conclusion to their meal. Brownies—I can smell them just hearing the word. These are the ultimate brownie, rich and chewy, with a hint of cinnamon from Mexican-style chocolate. Plop some ice cream alongside a generous brownie. I can't think of a better way to end a day in the snow.

Warm Spinach Salad with Honey Dijon Dressing

Dressing

¼ cup rice wine vinegar
¼ cup Dijon mustard
¼ cup honey
2 shallots, finely chopped
3 garlic cloves, finely chopped
¼ cup sesame oil
¾ cup vegetable oil
Salt and pepper to taste

Salad

2 bunches spinach, cleaned and torn into medium-size pieces
1 red onion, julienned
2 cups oyster mushrooms, sliced
1 red bell pepper, julienned

½ cup toasted, slivered almonds for garnish
Pickled ginger for garnish

To make the dressing: Mix vinegar, mustard, honey, shallots, and garlic in a medium-size mixing bowl. Slowly whisk in the oils to emulsify. Season with salt and pepper. This dressing will keep covered in your refrigerator up to 2 weeks.

To prepare the salad: Place cleaned spinach in a large mixing bowl. Heat onion, mushrooms, julienned pepper, and ¾ cup of dressing over medium heat in a sauté pan until the liquid boils. Pour over the spinach and toss. Garnish with toasted almonds and pickled ginger. Serve immediately.

Serves 6

Northwest Seafood Stew

Base

2 tablespoons unsalted butter

3 shallots, finely chopped

4 garlic cloves, finely chopped

1 medium onion, diced

3 stalks celery, diced

2 cups hearty, dry red wine

2 cups Shrimp Stock (see page 226)

1 large can (about 16 ounces) diced Roma tomatoes, or

2 pounds fresh tomatoes, peeled, seeded, and diced

1 teaspoon dried oregano

1 teaspoon dried basil

1 teaspoon dried thyme

Cracked black pepper and salt to taste

2 tablespoons olive oil

2 pounds mussels, washed and debearded

1 pound clams, rinsed

1 pound shrimp, peeled and deveined (save shells for stock)

1 pound seasonal whitefish, cut into small chunks

Toasted garlic croutons for garnish

To make soup base: Melt butter in a large stockpot, then add the shallots, garlic, and onion and sauté slightly over high heat. Add celery and sauté about 2 minutes. Add red wine and reduce liquid by half. Once wine has reduced, add stock and reduce by half again. Add diced Roma tomatoes and simmer for about 10 minutes. Add oregano, basil, and thyme, and season with salt and pepper. Keep warm, or remove from heat and freeze for later use.

To finish stew: In a large sauté pan, heat 2 tablespoons of olive oil on high heat until smoking hot. Place mussels and

clams in the pan and cook until the shellfish start to open
(about 2 to 3 minutes). Add the shrimp and sauté slightly.
Add the whitefish and sauté just long enough to cook the
outside of the fish. (If there isn't enough room in your sauté
pan, add fish directly to the soup base instead.) Add all the
seafood to the soup base. Serve hot, topped with toasted garlic
croutons.

Serves 6

HINT: Make a double batch of the soup base and freeze what
you don't use. If you're a garlic fan, try adding whole Roasted
Garlic cloves (see page 229) to the soup base.

The Ultimate Brownie

3 eggs
¾ cup sugar
1 teaspoon vanilla
½ cup butter
4 ounces Ibarra Mexican-style chocolate
¾ cup ground sweet chocolate
¾ cup flour
¼ teaspoon baking powder
Pinch of salt
1 cup toasted chopped pecans

Coffee ice cream or whipped cream (optional)

Preheat oven to 350 degrees.

Beat together eggs, sugar, and vanilla. Melt the butter in a small pan over medium to low heat. Stir in the Mexican chocolate, a small amount at a time, until melted. Cool slightly.

Stir ground chocolate, flour, baking powder, and salt into egg mixture. Once dry ingredients are totally blended, add the melted chocolate and butter.

Pour batter into a greased and floured 9-inch pie pan. Bake for 20 minutes (it should have a fudgelike consistency). Cut into 12 pieces. Serve warm, with coffee ice cream or whipped cream flavored with Grand Marnier.

Makes 12 brownies

NOTE: If you can't find Mexican chocolate in your local market, use regular bittersweet chocolate with ½ teaspoon cinnamon added.

91

STUFFED PORK LOIN DINNER FOR 4

One-Minute Salmon with Tarragon Butter Sauce

Warm Spinach Salad with
Cabernet Dressing and Herb Goat Cheese

Pork Loin with Hazelnut, Sausage,
and Wild Mushroom Stuffing

Ginger Angel Food Cake with Apricot Sauce

WINE SUGGESTION
Hogue Reserve Merlot

WHEN MY HUSBAND JOHN AND I have people over for dinner, everyone gets into the act. Of course, that may be because many of our friends are chefs. Even friends who aren't chefs get into the act, though. It's a warm feeling sharing the intimacy of creating a meal together. Since this menu requires more time in the kitchen, give everyone something to do and let the party begin.

The one-minute salmon is a recipe I adapted from one that was often used at the Shoalwater Restaurant at the Shelburne Inn in Seaview, Washington. I spent two memorable summers working there. My favorite aspect of this treatment is the way the salmon melts in your mouth. Coupled with a butter sauce, the salmon's texture is incredible. There are two things to remember when working with this recipe: keep the butter sauce at a constant temperature (these sauces don't like extremes), and don't overcook the salmon. Leave it in the oven just until it starts to turn pink.

A cabernet dressing, rich with wine and Oven Roasted Shallots, combines with the creamy tart flavors of mild goat cheese and tender spinach leaves to create a delicious salad. I warm the dressing in this recipe because the flavors stand out better when they've been heated. The dressing is poured over spinach leaves, tossed, and topped with a round of the goat cheese rolled in herbs. If you're eating light, this salad makes a perfect entree with a good loaf of crusty french bread.

Hearty pleasure for your winter dining arrives in the form of pork loin stuffed with sage, wild mushrooms, hazelnuts, and sausage, which adds the bit of fat needed to keep the pork moist. The stuffing can be made the day before or early in the day, but I would not stuff the pork until just before cooking it. The roast is wrapped in fresh herb sprigs to add a fragrant touch. It is also is a beautiful way to serve it.

Dessert for your co-cooks is an angel food cake. I remember how this cake was supposed to be too difficult to bother making. The egg whites had to be just so, and you had to have a special pan with a tube in the middle specially designed to hang upside down on a Coke bottle. You may be pleasantly surprised to discover that you have to remember only a few rules to master this cake: start with clean utensils, make sure the egg whites are clear (no yolk residue), and don't overbeat the whites when adding the flour and sugar. It is worth the effort because this dessert is healthy as well as tasty—it contains no egg yolks, butter fat, or any fat whatsoever. Except for the cream in the apricot sauce and the whipped cream on the side. (You can't always be good—it just wouldn't be dessert.)

One-Minute Salmon
with Tarragon Butter Sauce

Sauce

Juice of 1 lemon
2 tablespoons rice wine vinegar
¼ cup dry white wine
2 shallots, coarsely chopped
2 garlic cloves, coarsely chopped
½ pound unsalted butter
2 teaspoons finely chopped fresh tarragon
Salt and pepper to taste

2 pounds salmon fillets, skin removed
1 teaspoon unsalted butter

Fresh tarragon sprigs for garnish

Preheat oven to 350 degrees.

To make sauce: Place lemon juice, vinegar, wine, shallots, and garlic in a small saucepan. Over high heat, reduce liquid to 2 tablespoons. Lower heat to medium and slowly whisk in butter. Maintain mixture at a constant temperature; it will separate if it gets too hot or too cold. Strain through a fine strainer and add tarragon and salt and pepper. Keep warm but not hot.

To cook salmon: Slice salmon fillet at a 45-degree angle, as thinly as possible. Butter 4 medium-size, ovenproof salad plates. Place 3 slices of salmon on each plate; shape like a fan. Place plates in oven and cook about 1 minute or just until salmon starts to turn pink.

Remove plates from oven. Sauce the salmon and garnish with fresh tarragon. Serve hot.

Serves 4

95

Warm Spinach Salad with Cabernet Dressing and Herb Goat Cheese

Dressing
6 Oven Roasted Shallots (see page 229), coarsely chopped
2 garlic cloves, finely chopped
¼ cup cabernet wine vinegar
2 teaspoons Dijon mustard
½ teaspoon cracked black pepper
¾ cup extra virgin olive oil
Salt to taste

6 ounces mild soft goat cheese
2 teaspoons finely chopped fresh herbs (such as basil, savory, and marjoram)

2 bunches cleaned spinach, larger leaves torn into smaller pieces (small leaves can be left whole)

To make dressing: Place shallots, garlic, vinegar, mustard, and pepper in a medium-size mixing bowl. Slowly whisk in oil to emulsify. Add salt to taste.

Roll goat cheese in herbs to form a 2-inch-thick log. Slice into 4 circles and reserve.

Place spinach leaves in a large bowl. In a medium-size sauté pan, heat dressing over high heat until it just reaches a boil. Pour over spinach and toss. Place spinach on salad plates and top with a goat cheese round.

Serves 4

Pork Loin with Hazelnut, Sausage, and Wild Mushroom Stuffing

1 tablespoon vegetable oil

1 small onion, diced

2 garlic cloves, chopped

¼ pound wild mushrooms (such as oyster and shiitake)

3 ounces pork sausage

¼ cup toasted, chopped hazelnuts

1 teaspoon chopped fresh sage

1½ pounds boned pork loin

1 bunch each rosemary, thyme, and marjoram

2 tablespoons vegetable oil

Preheat oven to 425 degrees.

Heat oil in a small sauté pan over high heat. Add onion and garlic, and sauté lightly. Add sliced mushroom and sauté until tender. Cool onion mixture. Place in a medium-size mixing bowl with sausage, hazelnuts, and sage. Mix well.

Butterfly pork loin, following the grain. Spread sausage mixture evenly on pork loin. Roll the loin like a jelly roll. Place sprigs of rosemary, thyme, and marjoram along the top of the loin, and tie tightly with butcher's twine, spacing ties about 1 inch apart.

Heat 2 tablespoons vegetable oil in a large roasting pan, until smoking hot. Sear roast well on all sides. Transfer pan to oven and finish cooking, about 30 to 40 minutes for medium doneness.

Remove from the oven and let stand 3 to 4 minutes before slicing. Serve hot.

Serves 4

97

Ginger Angel Food Cake
with Apricot Sauce

Cake

1½ cups sugar

1 cup cake flour

¼ teaspoon salt

½ teaspoon ground ginger

1 tablespoon finely chopped crystallized ginger

16 large egg whites

2 teaspoons cream of tartar

2 teaspoons vanilla

Sauce

1 cup coarsely chopped dried apricots

1 cup late-harvest Riesling

½ cup sugar

1 cup heavy cream

Powdered sugar for dusting

Whipped cream for garnish

Fresh mint sprigs for garnish

Preheat oven to 350 degrees.

To make cake: In a small bowl combine ¾ cup sugar, flour, salt, and gingers. In a large mixing bowl, beat egg whites until soft peaks form. Gradually add the other ¾ cup of sugar and cream of tartar. Continue beating to stiff peaks. Carefully fold in vanilla and flour mixture, a bit at a time.

Pour batter into a greased and floured cake pan (can be any shape deep pan: tube, bundt, or loaf). Bake about 40 minutes, or until a knife inserted comes out clean. Remove from oven and cool completely, setting pan upside down.

To make sauce: Place apricots, wine, and sugar in a heavy saucepan and cook over medium heat until apricots are plump and soft. Puree with heavy cream until very smooth.

Serve angel food cake topped with apricot sauce and softly whipped cream. Dust with powdered sugar and garnish with mint.

Makes 1 cake

Winter Vegetable Salad

Oyster Stew

Herb Biscuits

Apple Crisp with Almond Crust

WINE SUGGESTION
Facelli Fumé Blanc

HOT, CREAMY OYSTER STEW, served with salad and homemade biscuits, and finished off with an updated version of old-fashioned apple crisp is a great menu to treat a few close friends to on a slow winter afternoon.

The vegetable salad tosses together some crisp and tasty vegetables—celeriac, carrots, jicama, leeks, and red onion. Dressed with a spicy Crème Fraîche, they are a wonderful match for the creaminess of oyster stew. I cut the vegetables julienne style, because I like the crunchiness of matchstick-sized vegetables. If you prefer your vegetables cut in bigger chunks, however, I suggest that you blanch them lightly.

The salad seems to have much more flavor when prepared several hours ahead of time because the seasonings have time to blend properly. Oyster stew, on the other hand, is best made just before eating. If you cook it too far ahead, the oysters will overcook and end up chewy and tough. Since I always prefer fresh ingredients, I suggest you buy oysters in the shell. The biscuits that accompany the stew can be made with a combination of any of your favorite herbs. They, too, can be made earlier and warmed before serving.

The afternoon's comforts are rounded out by a simple old-fashioned dessert based on a recipe my husband's mother makes. The smell of baking apples and spices conjures up happy memories of weekends I spent cooking at my in-laws' home while my husband, John, and I were still in cooking school in upstate New York. In this adaptation of a family recipe, I use crisp, tart Granny Smith apples. They are common and should be widely available. Almonds have been added to the traditional crust, but you can substitute any other nuts. Such a homey dessert will brighten and warm any chilly winter afternoon.

Winter Vegetable Salad

2 celeriacs, julienned
5 carrots, julienned
1 jicama, julienned
3 leeks, julienned
1 red onion, julienned
3 shallots, finely chopped
4 garlic cloves, finely chopped
2 tablespoons finely chopped gingerroot
1 teaspoon orange zest
Pinch of cayenne
1 cup Crème Fraîche (see page 230)
Salt and pepper to taste

Place julienned vegetables in a medium-size mixing bowl and toss. In a small mixing bowl, mix together shallots, garlic, ginger, orange zest, cayenne, Crème Fraîche, and salt and pepper. Pour Crème Fraîche mixture over vegetables and toss well. Refrigerate until ready to serve.

102

Serves 4

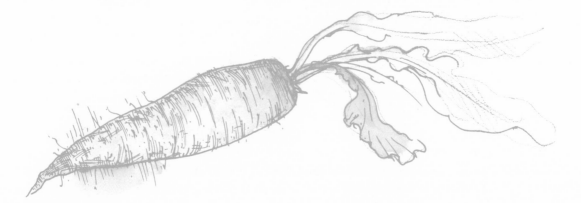

Oyster Stew

4 shallots, finely chopped
2 garlic cloves, finely chopped
2 leeks, halved lengthwise and julienned
3 tablespoons unsalted butter
½ cup dry sherry
¼ cup dry white wine
½ pound shucked fresh oysters
4 cups heavy cream
½ teaspoon finely chopped fresh thyme
Salt and pepper to taste

Fresh thyme sprigs for garnish

Over high heat, lightly sauté the shallots, garlic, and leeks in butter in a very large sauté pan. When you can smell the aroma of the onions and garlic, add the sherry and wine. Reduce by half.

Add the oysters and cream. Lower heat to medium and bring to a boil. Remove from heat, add fresh thyme, and season with salt and pepper.

Place soup in warm bowls and garnish with fresh sprigs of thyme.

Serves 4

103

Herb Biscuits

2 cups flour
1 tablespoon baking powder
2 tablespoons wheat germ
2 tablespoons grated Parmesan cheese
1 tablespoon chopped, mixed fresh herbs
 (such as tarragon, basil, and marjoram)
1 teaspoon salt
¼ cup shortening
½ cup milk
¼ cup buttermilk

Preheat oven to 425 degrees.

In a large bowl, combine the flour, baking powder, wheat germ, Parmesan cheese, herbs, and salt. Blend shortening into the dry ingredient mixture until it resembles coarse crumbs. Add milk and buttermilk. Stir with a fork just until the mixture comes together.

Turn the dough onto a floured surface and knead 1 minute. Roll dough out to ½-inch thickness. Use a 2-inch round cookie cutter to cut out the biscuits. Bake on a lightly greased baking sheet for 15 minutes or until golden brown. Serve warm.

Makes 1 dozen biscuits

Apple Crisp with Almond Crust

Crust

½ cup ground toasted almonds

1⅓ cups flour

½ cup powdered sugar

1 cup unsalted butter, softened

1 teaspoon salt

½ teaspoon almond extract

Filling

5 Granny Smith apples, peeled, cored, and sliced

¼ cup brown sugar

¼ cup sugar

⅓ cup brandy

1 tablespoon unsalted butter, softened

1 teaspoon cinnamon

½ teaspoon vanilla

Whipped cream or vanilla ice cream

Preheat oven to 350 degrees.

To make the crust: Place the toasted almonds, flour, and powdered sugar in a medium-size mixing bowl. Add butter, salt, and almond extract and mix until dough begins to come together (do not mix until smooth). Reserve.

To make the filling: Toss the sliced apples with the brown sugar, sugar, brandy, butter, cinnamon, and vanilla. Place the filling in a lightly buttered 9-inch pie pan and crumble the almond crust dough over it, covering well.

Bake for 40 minutes or until golden brown and crispy. Serve warm with whipped cream or vanilla ice cream.

Serves 4

GRILLED SALMON LUNCHEON FOR 4

Winter Squash Soup with Orange and Sage

Grilled Salmon with Dried Cranberry Aïoli

Dennis's Chocolate Swirl Bread Pudding

WINE SUGGESTION
Chalone Pinot Noir

W INTER, SPRING, SUMMER, OR fall, John and I use our grill as long as it's not raining or snowing. The grilled salmon entree in this menu can be served hot or chilled, with a tangy aïoli that is flavored by plumped, dried cranberries and fresh thyme. The cranberries add both tart and sweet flavors to the sauce, which complements the richness of the salmon. Served on a bed of greens, this dish also makes a great entree salad.

In the squash soup, I used Duck Stock because it adds a nice complexity. Additionally, fresh sage, orange zest, and the pleasing nuttiness of sherry make this satisfying enough to serve as an entree. For a special dinner at Fullers, we once served this soup in bowls carved out of small pumpkins. It was a big hit.

I must confess that the only contribution I have made to this menu's bread pudding is to have written it down. Dennis Chun, a wonderful gentleman who runs Fullers's *garde manger* station (cold entrees, salads, desserts, and appetizers) during lunch, gets the credit for this dessert. He has a natural gift for food. This bread pudding, like most of his desserts, was the result of just fiddling around with a recipe. With its layering of day-old croissants, vanilla, and a fudge chocolate custard, this is one of the best bread puddings I've ever tasted—especially served warm.

Winter Squash Soup with Orange and Sage

2 tablespoons unsalted butter

1 medium onion, diced

3 shallots, chopped

3 garlic cloves, chopped

2 pounds winter squash, peeled and diced

2 carrots, peeled and diced

½ teaspoon orange zest

1 cup sherry

1 quart Duck Stock (see page 227)

2 cups heavy cream

1 teaspoon finely chopped fresh sage

Salt and pepper to taste

Heat butter in a large saucepan on high heat, and lightly sauté onions, shallots, and garlic. Add squash, carrots, zest, and sherry. Reduce by half. Add stock and cook until squash is tender. Puree soup in a food processor and pour back into pan. Add cream, sage, salt, and pepper. Serve hot.

108

Serves 4

Grilled Salmon with Dried Cranberry Aïoli

Aïoli

½ cup dried cranberries
1 cup red wine
3 shallots, chopped
5 garlic cloves, chopped
3 egg yolks
¼ cup red wine vinegar
½ teaspoon dry mustard
3 cups vegetable oil
1 teaspoon finely chopped fresh thyme
Salt and pepper to taste

4 4-ounce salmon fillets
2 tablespoons vegetable oil
Salt and pepper to taste

To make aïoli: Place cranberries in a small saucepan with red wine. Cook over high heat until cranberries are soft and plumped. Puree and reserve. Place garlic, shallots, yolks, vinegar, and dry mustard in a mixing bowl. Mix well. Slowly whisk in oil to emulsify, then add thyme and puree. Season with salt and pepper to taste. Refrigerate until needed.

To cook salmon: Brush salmon fillets with oil and season with salt and pepper. Place fillets on grill and cook about 4 to 5 minutes, depending on the size of the fillet. Remove salmon from grill and serve hot or cold, with the aïoli on top or on the side.

Serves 4

109

Dennis's Chocolate Swirl Bread Pudding

1 cup sour cream
3 whole eggs, slightly beaten
2 teaspoons salt
1 cup buttermilk
8 ounces semisweet chocolate
1 cup half-and-half
12 small croissants, day old
¾ cup butter, melted

Preheat oven to 350 degrees. Prepare warm-water bath of ¼ inch of water in a large baking pan.

In a small mixing bowl, combine sour cream, eggs, salt, and buttermilk. Mix well and reserve.

Over boiling water, melt chocolate with the half-and-half in a metal bowl. Remove from heat, mix well, and reserve.

Grease a 10-inch round cake pan. Slice the croissants lengthwise into ¼-inch slices. Line the bottom of the cake pan with half the croissant slices and drizzle half the melted butter over them. Pour half the egg-and-sour-cream mixture over the croissants, then drizzle half the chocolate mixture over that. Using a knife, swirl the two mixtures together until they are marbled.

Repeat with another layer of croissant slices, butter, and the two mixtures. Marble again.

Set in water bath and bake for 1½ hours, or until a knife inserted comes out clean. Serve warm.

Serves 4

110

POACHED EGGS AND SPICY HASH
FOR 4

Poached Eggs

Spicy Corned Beef Hash with
Roasted Red Pepper Puree

THIS BREAKFAST IS HEARTY AND spicy—a great meal to serve before heading for the ski slopes. I've taken an old-fashioned hash and spiked it with jalapeño, then topped it with poached eggs and a roasted red pepper sauce.

When poaching the eggs, be careful not to let the poaching liquid come to a boil while the eggs are cooking. They will break apart and become rubbery. They also become rubbery if overcooked. I also suggest you break eggs into a cup before putting them in the poaching liquid. This allows you to check that the yolk is intact and doesn't contain any blood spots.

The sauce that tops the eggs and hash is simple, but the roasted red peppers give it a great robust flavor. A bit of vinegar gives it a tartness, and chili powder adds spice. If you would like the sauce even hotter, add half a fresh jalapeño (remove the seeds) while pureeing the peppers. Hot or mild, this breakfast will fuel an active day.

Poached Eggs

1 quart water
1 tablespoon white wine vinegar
8 large eggs

Place water and vinegar in a flat saucepan and bring to a boil. Once boiling, lower heat and simmer. Break eggs into cups before placing in poaching liquid. This will ensure that you do not break the yolks before poaching. Pour eggs from the cups into the water. Cook just until whites are set, about 3 to 5 minutes. Remove with a slotted spoon and drain well.

Serves 4

Spicy Corned Beef Hash with Roasted Red Pepper Puree

4 medium new potatoes, diced large
1 small onion, diced small
1 small carrot, diced small
1 rib celery, diced small
1 to 1½ pounds cooked corned beef
3 tablespoons vegetable oil
6 ounces chili sauce
2 garlic cloves, finely chopped
1 small jalapeño pepper, finely chopped
Roasted Red Pepper Puree (recipe follows)

Blanch potatoes, cool, and reserve.

In a food processor fitted with a metal blade, place onion, carrot, celery, and corned beef; pulse until coarsely chopped. Reserve.

Heat oil in a large nonstick sauté pan. Brown potatoes in hot oil. Add chili sauce, garlic, and jalapeño to vegetable-and-corned-beef mixture, mix well, and transfer to pan with potatoes. Stir to mix well, then flatten with a spatula to form a large pancake. Brown well, then flip and brown the other side.

Remove from pan and cut into quarters. Place each wedge on a plate, top with 2 poached eggs, and drizzle Roasted Red Pepper Puree over both.

Serves 4

114

Roasted Red Pepper Puree

2 red bell peppers
2 tablespoons olive oil
1 tablespoon sherry vinegar
Pinch of cumin
Pinch of chili powder
Salt and pepper to taste

Rub peppers with a bit of the olive oil and roast in 500-degree oven (or about 4 inches under the broiler) until skins become blistered and black. Remove from the oven; cover for about 5 minutes with a towel.

When peppers are cool, remove skin (it will slip off easily), seeds, and stems. Place peppers, olive oil, sherry vinegar, and spices in a blender or food processor. Blend until smooth.

Makes about ½ cup

115

WINTER BREAKFAST FOR 6

Apple Apricot Coffee Cake Braid

Seafood Sausages

Swiss Potatoes

Passion Fruit Mimosas

THIS MENU MAKES A WONDERFUL weekend breakfast (or brunch for those of you who like to sleep late). Even non-morning people might be tempted to rise a little early when they smell this apple apricot coffee cake baking. The recipe for the coffee cake dough makes a large batch, so you can make one braid and freeze half the dough for another time. To work with frozen dough, take it out the night before and allow it to thaw slowly (in the refrigerator), then fill and bake it in the morning.

The Seafood Sausage is a recipe I adapted from one that originally came from the American Regional restaurant at the Culinary Institute of America. There, this dish was served as a dinner appetizer, but I like the sausage at breakfast instead. I also added fresh thyme and diced red bell peppers to the original recipe. The sausages can be made several days ahead of time and stored in your refrigerator until the morning you use them. When selecting the seafood, look for scallops that are firm and not too large. The whitefish flesh should be firm and free of gouges and blood spots.

The Swiss potatoes are my husband John's recipe. They are my favorite breakfast potatoes, and anyone who has ever eaten them at our house pleads for them on return visits. The taste and texture of this dish depend on a golden crispy crust, so it is important to be sure the potatoes are well-browned on one side before flipping them to cook the other side. A good-quality, well-marbled smoked bacon makes a big difference in this dish. You can also try bacon with cracked black pepper on the rind.

To enliven this winter breakfast, serve champagne. It's even more refreshing with the fresh orange juice and passion fruit nectar added. Try this drink while opening presents on Christmas morning.

Apple Apricot Coffee Cake Braid

Sweet Dough (makes 2 braids)
⅓ ounce dry active yeast
½ cup sugar
1 teaspoon salt
5 cups flour
1 teaspoon orange zest
½ cup unsalted butter
1 cup milk

Filling (fills 1 braid)
2 large Granny Smith apples, peeled, cored, and thinly sliced
1 cup toasted, coarsely chopped pecans
⅓ cup coarsely diced dried apricots
½ cup sugar
1 teaspoon vanilla
1 teaspoon cinnamon
½ teaspoon allspice
¼ teaspoon ground ginger
¼ teaspoon ground cloves

1 egg yolk
2 tablespoons water

Glaze (for 1 braid)
½ cup powdered sugar
¼ teaspoon vanilla
2 tablespoons orange juice concentrate

To prepare the dough: Place yeast, sugar, salt, 1 cup of flour, and orange zest in a large mixing bowl. Heat the butter and milk together in small saucepan until very hot—about 120 to 140 degrees—but do not allow to boil (the butter does not have to melt completely). Pour milk into the dry ingredients and mix to form a soft dough. Mix in remaining flour until the dough is not too sticky to handle. Knead on a well-floured board for 10 minutes until dough is smooth and elastic.

Place dough in a large, oiled mixing bowl, cover with a kitchen towel, and allow to rise in a warm place until doubled in size. Once doubled, punch the dough down and cut in half. Wrap and freeze one half; allow the other half to rest 10 to 15 minutes before filling and shaping.

To prepare the filling: Place the sliced apples in a medium-size mixing bowl with the pecans, apricots, sugar, vanilla, and spices. Toss together until well mixed. Reserve.

To prepare braid: Preheat oven to 350 degrees.

On a well-floured board, roll the sweet dough out to a 12-inch-by-14-inch rectangle, ¼ inch thick. Spread the filling down the middle of the dough in a 4-inch-wide strip. Along the sides of the dough, cut 1-inch-wide strips perpendicular to the filling. Fold the strips over the filling, alternating them to look like a braid. Place the braid on a greased baking sheet, cover with a towel, and allow to rise in a warm place for 1 hour or until doubled in size.

Before baking, brush the dough with egg yolk and water that have been whisked together. Bake 30 to 40 minutes or until golden brown.

To glaze, mix the sugar, vanilla, and orange juice concentrate together until smooth. Drizzle it over the cooled coffee cake.

Dough makes 2 braids; filling makes 1 braid

Seafood Sausages

¾ pound sea scallops
½ pound halibut or other mild whitefish
3 shallots, finely chopped
2 garlic cloves, finely chopped
1 cup heavy cream
4 large shrimp, diced
¼ pound crabmeat
1 teaspoon finely chopped chives
½ red bell pepper, diced small
1 teaspoon finely chopped fresh thyme
Salt and pepper to taste
Flour for dusting
2 tablespoons vegetable oil
Fresh herbs (tarragon or thyme) and red bell pepper,
    diced small, for garnish

Place bowl and blade of your food processor in the freezer to cool. Dice the scallops and whitefish (be sure to keep the seafood cold at all times when you're not working with it). Once the food processor is cold, place fish, scallops, shallots, and garlic in the bowl and puree until smooth. Do not overwork the fish.

Stop the motor and scrape down the sides well. With the motor running, slowly add the cream. Once all the cream is added, remove fish mixture and place in a medium-size mixing bowl set in a larger mixing bowl filled with ice. Fold in the shrimp, crab, chives, red pepper, fresh thyme, and seasonings to make a mousse.

Fill a large pastry bag fitted with a large plain tube with the seafood mousse. Pipe the mixture lengthwise down the middle of a sheet of plastic wrap about 50 inches long. Fold the plastic wrap in half over the mousse, then roll the mousse over to cover with excess wrap.

With butcher's twine, tie one end of wrapped mousse. Approximately every 5 inches, tie again to form sausages, then secure the other end with another piece of twine.

In a large stockpot, heat about 2 inches of water to a simmer. Set the sausage roll in the water and poach it for 6 to 8 minutes or until firm to the touch. Let the sausage roll cool after removing from the water, then unwrap the roll and dust the individual sausage links lightly with flour. Sauté in vegetable oil over high heat until golden brown. Garnish with fresh herbs and diced red peppers. Serve immediately.

Serves 6

NOTE: When preparing the fish mousse, it is very important that all ingredients stay cold so the mousse won't separate. If the mixture feels like it is getting too warm, place it in the refrigerator for 5 minutes or put it back on ice in a larger bowl.

Other garnishes for the sausages can be almost anything—lobster meat, mussels, or wild mushrooms are all good.

121

Swiss Potatoes

5 medium potatoes
5 bacon strips, diced
1 small onion, sliced
2 tablespoons butter, melted
Salt and pepper to taste
½ cup sour cream
½ cup grated Gouda cheese

Boil potatoes in a large saucepan until fork tender. Drain and cool, then grate.

In a large nonstick sauté pan, sauté the bacon until crisp. Add onions and sauté until soft. Add the grated potatoes and mix well with the onions and bacon. Using a spatula, shape the potato mixture to form a pancake. Brush the top of the potato pancake with butter. Cook over medium heat until bottom is brown. Season with salt and pepper, flip pancake, and brown the other side.

Remove from pan, cut into six wedges, and top with sour cream and grated Gouda.

Serves 6

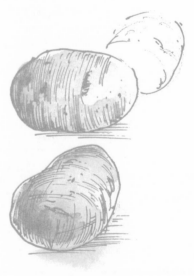

Passion Fruit Mimosas

6 ounces passion fruit nectar
1 bottle champagne
Fresh orange juice
Fresh mint and mango slices for garnish

Pour 1 ounce of passion fruit nectar in the bottom of 6 well-chilled champagne flutes. Fill glasses three-quarters full with champagne. Top off glasses with fresh orange juice and garnish with fresh mint and a mango slice.

Serves 6

SPRING

Marinated Chinese Noodles

Curried Mussels

Cardamom Orange Ice Cream

In March 1989 I was invited to Malaysia to cook a birthday dinner for a sultan. It was quite an honor, but what was really exciting was the chance to experience Malaysian cuisine. Kuala Lumpur is a city of ethnic diversity—Chinese, Indian, and Malaysian. While I was there, a young Chinese boy befriended me and took me on a tour of small shops with dried fish and open-air stalls, where noodles and fish balls are made while you wait. The tastes and smells from this trip have filtered into my cooking, as you will see in this menu. It features ingredients commonly found in Asian cuisines—sesame oil, soy sauce, curry, and cardamom.

The Chinese Noodles are flavored with soy sauce and sesame oil. This is a dish that benefits from being made the day before; the flavors become much stronger when the noodles are allowed to marinate. If you eat them cold, right out of the refrigerator, the noodles can be tough and the sesame flavors hidden—so be sure to serve them at room temperature.

As in many Asian dishes, the curried mussels are quick and easy to prepare. Except for mincing a bit of garlic and ginger, there is little to do but throw everything together in a large pot and steam it for a few minutes. Juices from the shellfish, sake, and curry produce a spicy broth that is a wonderful complement to the mussels.

Since this menu reflects the taste of Asia, I finish it with some creamy cardamom ice cream with just a hint of orange. Cardamom, a member of the ginger family, is a spice native to southern Asia, primarily India and Sri Lanka. Cardamom and orange and other citrus flavors are common to many Asian foods, especially desserts. The ice cream is even better topped with fresh seasonal berries.

Marinated Chinese Noodles

½ pound dry Chinese egg noodles
3 tablespoons plus 1 teaspoon peanut oil
2 garlic cloves, finely chopped
½ teaspoon chile flakes
2 tablespoons soy sauce
3 tablespoons sesame oil

Cook egg noodles in about 2 quarts of salted water about 5 minutes, or until tender or *al dente*. Drain and toss with 1 teaspoon peanut oil to keep noodles from sticking. In a small bowl, combine garlic, chile flakes, soy sauce, remaining peanut oil, and sesame oil. Mix well and toss with noodles. Serve at room temperature.

Serves 4

HINT: I toss the noodles with the dressing while they are warm because I feel the flavors are stronger when heated first and then allowed to cool to room temperature.

Curried Mussels

6 pounds mussels, cleaned and debearded
1 teaspoon finely chopped gingerroot
3 shallots, finely chopped
3 garlic cloves, finely chopped
1 cup sake
Juice of 1 lime
½ pound unsalted butter
2 teaspoons good-quality curry powder

Pickled ginger and cilantro for garnish

Place mussels in a very large stockpot (preferably a wide, flat pot). Add all other ingredients except garnish and steam over high heat just until mussels open. Distribute mussels into 4 large bowls. Pour liquid over mussels and garnish with a bit of pickled ginger and cilantro.

Serves 4

129

HINT: It is a good idea to dry sauté the curry before adding it to any recipe. To do this, place curry in a small sauté pan. Heat pan and curry until hot, and toss to roast a bit (2 or 3 minutes). Cool.

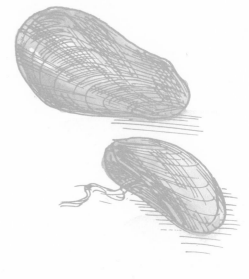

Cardamom Orange Ice Cream

1 quart half-and-half
1 cup sugar
6 egg yolks
½ teaspoon crushed cardamom
Pinch of ground ginger
1 tablespoon orange zest

Mint sprigs and fortune cookies for garnish

In a heavy-bottomed saucepan, over medium heat, combine half-and-half and ½ cup of sugar and cook just until it boils. In a small bowl, mix egg yolks and the rest of the sugar. Temper the yolks by slowly adding a bit of hot half-and-half. Once the yolk mixture is heated, stir it into the half-and-half and cook over low to medium heat until the mixture coats the back of a spoon. Do not boil.

Remove mixture from heat and add cardamom, ginger, and orange zest. Cool completely. Freeze in an ice-cream maker, following the manufacturer's directions. Garnish with a bit of mint and a fortune cookie.

Makes 1½ quarts

POACHED SALMON DINNER FOR 6

Chilled Asparagus Soup

Early Spring Lettuces Tossed with Sorrel and
Lemon Vinaigrette

Oven-Poached Salmon with Tarragon and Crispy
Shallot Butter

Strawberry Rhubarb Tart with Chocolate Crust

Spring fever sometimes takes hold of me as early as the middle of February. When the sun breaks though what seem like endless days of clouds and rain, I start to think about working in my yard and I yearn for fresh local produce. By the time March arrives, I can barely wait until April, when—finally—the first of the local spring produce starts to arrive. Baby lettuce, field greens, and edible flowers—this dinner menu celebrates these first sproutings.

Pencil-thin asparagus flavors this soup, with some spears saved for a garnish. When you buy asparagus, look for firm stalks that are smooth and not wrinkled. The spears should be tightly closed, not budding. The soup can be made days ahead, and it will store in the freezer for several months. Those of you who live where spring weather is fickle will appreciate that this soup can be served hot or cold.

An herb I associate with spring—sorrel—flavors the salad dressing. Although it is available nearly year-round, sorrel is best at this time of year, when its new shoots are tender. Its delicate, citrusy flavor is a delightful accompaniment to the tiny individual heads of early spring lettuce featured in this salad. Sorrel can be fragile and browns very easily, so watch for leaves that are turning color or look old.

Fresh salmon, oven poached in a small amount of wine, is the entree. The salmon is accompanied by a light butter sauce, which combines fresh tarragon with roasted shallots. Although a butter sauce may not be low in calories, its lightness is in the way it sits in your mouth. The butter rounds out the more delicate, crisper flavors, making this type of sauce just right for a spring meal.

To conclude the meal, I have varied an old standard—strawberry and rhubarb pie—by adding chocolate to the crust. This is the way I finish a meal with a light, yet decadent touch. Here's to spring!

Chilled Asparagus Soup

1 pound fresh asparagus (steam and set aside ¼ of tips
*   for garnish)*
1 medium yellow onion, diced
3 garlic cloves, chopped
4 shallots, chopped
2 tablespoons unsalted butter
2 potatoes, peeled and diced
1 pint Chicken Stock (see page 227)
2 cups heavy cream
Salt and pepper to taste

Sprig of fresh herbs for garnish (lemon thyme and tarragon)

Blanch a quarter of the asparagus tips, chill in ice water, and reserve for garnish. Sauté onion, garlic, and shallots in butter in a large, heavy saucepan over high heat until tender. Add potatoes, remaining asparagus, and Chicken Stock. Simmer until the potatoes are soft, then transfer to a blender or food processor and puree. Return soup to the saucepan, add the cream, and heat just until it boils. Remove from heat and cool.

Serve chilled, garnished with asparagus tips and a sprig of fresh herbs.

Serves 6

VARIATIONS: Add fresh herbs, such as thyme or even mint, to this soup. If you are trying to cut down on calories, reduce the amount of cream by half, or use half-and-half instead. You can reheat this soup and serve it warm.

133

Early Spring Lettuces Tossed with Sorrel and Lemon Vinaigrette

Vinaigrette

¼ cup champagne vinegar
3 shallots, finely chopped
2 garlic cloves, finely chopped
1 teaspoon lemon zest
2 tablespoons Dijon mustard
1 tablespoon finely chopped sorrel
¼ cup extra virgin olive oil
½ cup vegetable oil
Salt and pepper to taste

Salad

18 heads of spring baby lettuce
1 small cucumber, thinly sliced
6 radishes, thinly sliced

134

To make the vinaigrette: In a medium-size mixing bowl, mix together vinegar, shallots, garlic, lemon zest, mustard, and chopped sorrel. Slowly whisk in oils, one at a time, making sure to emulsify the dressing. Season with salt and pepper. Store in refrigerator until ready to use (will keep up to 2 weeks).

To prepare the salad: On individual chilled plates, arrange 3 heads of washed, whole baby lettuces and top with cucumber and radish slices. Drizzle vinaigrette over each salad and serve.

Serves 6

VARIATIONS: Try orange or lime zest instead of lemon for a different twist on the dressing. Another variation is to use a green-peppercorn-flavored mustard instead of Dijon.

Oven-Poached Salmon with Tarragon and Crispy Shallot Butter

Sauce
½ cup white wine
½ cup sherry
3 shallots, chopped
2 garlic cloves, chopped
¼ cup tarragon vinegar
1 pound unsalted butter
Salt and pepper to taste
1 teaspoon finely chopped tarragon sprigs

Shallots
2 tablespoons vegetable oil
3 shallots, coarsely chopped

Poached Salmon
6 6-ounce salmon fillets
1 cup white wine
1 tablespoon butter
Salt and pepper to taste

Sprigs of fresh tarragon and edible flowers for garnish

To make the sauce: In a heavy saucepan over high heat, combine wine, sherry, shallots, garlic, tarragon sprigs, and vinegar and reduce to about ¼ cup of liquid. Lower heat to medium and slowly whisk in butter, making sure that the mixture maintains an even heat and does not get too cool or too hot. Season with salt and pepper. Strain and reserve, keeping warm (not hot).

To cook the shallots: In a sauté pan over high heat, heat oil and add shallots. Caramelize shallots until very brown and crispy (about 3 to 5 minutes). Stir into reserved sauce.

135

To poach the salmon: Preheat oven to 350 degrees. Place the fillets in a baking pan. Pour wine over the fillets and dot with butter. Season with salt and pepper. Bake about 10 minutes in oven. Do not overcook or the fish will become dry. Remove from pan and drain.

To serve: Distribute roasted shallot butter sauce evenly on plates. Place salmon fillets on sauced plates and garnish with fresh sprigs of tarragon and edible flowers.

Serves 6

VARIATIONS: Try adding ½ cup fresh orange juice and ½ teaspoon zest to change the flavor of the sauce. Bake the salmon with sprigs of fresh herbs and orange and lemon slices. This method adds a lot of flavor to the fish.

Strawberry Rhubarb Tart with Chocolate Crust

Crust

1 cup unsalted butter
½ cup powdered sugar
2 cups flour
2 tablespoons cocoa powder
1 teaspoon vanilla
½ teaspoon salt

Filling

1 pound rhubarb, diced small
1 cup sugar
2 teaspoons orange zest
Pinch of ground ginger
1 pint strawberries, cleaned, hulled, and quartered

To make the crust: In food processor, cream butter and powdered sugar. Once butter is softened, stop machine and add flour, cocoa powder, vanilla, and salt. Process again until mixture forms a ball. If dough becomes too soft, refrigerate for 1 hour. Press dough into ungreased flan pan, making sure it is pressed evenly over bottom and sides. Refrigerate until ready to fill.

Preheat oven to 350 degrees.

To make filling: Place rhubarb, sugar, zest, and ginger in a large mixing bowl. Add strawberries and toss well. Spread mixture into prepared crust. Bake about 30 minutes, or until rhubarb is very tender. Serve warm.

Serves 6

137

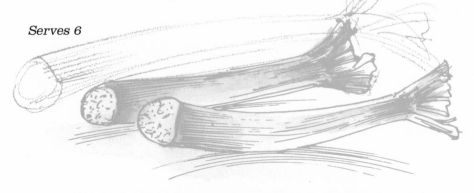

SAUTÉED HALIBUT LUNCH FOR 4

Chilled Carrot Soup
with Coconut Poached Prawns

Sautéed Halibut with Green Peppercorn
and Grilled Scallion Aïoli

Mocha Bean Cookies

ONCE WARMER WEATHER SETS IN, we turn to lighter and simpler foods and techniques. Instead of braising and roasting, we are more likely to grill or sauté our meats and seafoods. This menu reflects the natural shift from the hearty dishes of winter to the lighter, fresh fare of the warm days ahead.

The soup that begins this meal could easily serve as an entree, with its sweet mix of carrots and prawns, poached in coconut milk. To deepen the flavor, they are left in the liquid to cool. Make sure not to overcook the prawns, because they continue to cook while cooling down. You can make this soup well before lunch and add the prawns at the last moment.

Fresh halibut starts to appear in Northwest fish markets in the spring. In this treatment, I sauté this mild fish and top it with a spicy aïoli. Aïoli is a mayonnaise base laced with a heavy dose of garlic. This one has the added bite of green peppercorns and grilled scallions. Halibut should be cooked just until it's slightly opaque in the middle, medium rare (overcooked halibut will be dry and tough).

I love dessert, but I don't always want something heavy, such as a torte or cake. Sometimes just a cookie will do. These are somewhat like chocolate chip cookies, but with coffee-flavored, chocolate mocha beans. You can find these confections at specialty coffee stores. You could also make the cookies with a combination of mocha beans and white chocolate chips. However you alter them, the best way to eat them is warm, right out of the oven, accompanied by a dark, foamy caffe latte.

Chilled Carrot Soup
with Coconut Poached Prawns

Soup Base

2 tablespoons unsalted butter

3 shallots, finely chopped

3 garlic cloves, finely chopped

4 carrots, peeled and diced large

1 large russet potato, peeled and diced large

1 pint Chicken Stock (see page 227)

1 cup heavy cream

Salt and pepper to taste

Poached Prawns

1 14-ounce can coconut milk

½ cup water

Juice of 1 lime

1 teaspoon grated gingerroot

12 medium prawns, peeled and deveined

Sprigs of fresh cilantro for garnish

To make the soup base: In a large saucepan, heat the butter and add shallots and garlic. Sauté on high heat until you can smell the aroma of the garlic and shallots. Add the diced carrots and potato and sauté just long enough to coat them with butter.

Add Chicken Stock to the sautéed vegetables and reduce by half. Add cream and again reduce by half. Season with salt and pepper. Transfer to a blender or food processor and puree. Chill.

To poach the prawns: Place coconut milk, water, lime juice, and ginger in a medium-size saucepan and bring to a boil. Add prawns and cook just until they turn pink. Remove from heat and cool prawns in the liquid. Remove cooled prawns from poaching liquid and dice. Add to chilled carrot soup. Garnish with fresh cilantro and serve.

Serves 4

VARIATIONS: Substitute 1 cup orange juice for 1 cup of the Chicken Stock to change the flavor of the soup. Also try adding 1 teaspoon finely chopped gingerroot to the soup base.

Sautéed Halibut with Green Peppercorn and Grilled Scallion Aïoli

Aïoli

3 scallions, diced
⅛ cup sherry vinegar
2 shallots, finely chopped
4 garlic cloves, finely chopped
1 egg yolk
1 tablespoon Dijon mustard
¾ cup vegetable oil
½ teaspoon chopped green peppercorns
Salt and pepper to taste

2 tablespoons vegetable oil
4 6-ounce halibut fillets
Salt and pepper to taste

Sliced scallions for garnish

142

   To make aïoli: Grill diced scallions in lightly oiled sauté pan over high heat until just lightly browned. Reserve.

   Place vinegar, shallots, garlic, egg yolk, and mustard in a medium-size bowl. Slowly whisk in oil to emulsify. Add chopped peppercorns and grilled scallions, and mix well. Season with salt and pepper. Refrigerate.

   To cook fish: In a very large sauté pan, heat oil over high heat until smoking hot. Place the halibut in the pan and sear each side well. Continue to cook another 3 to 5 minutes, or until a knife inserted in the middle of the fish feels warm, not hot or cold, when you pull it out.

   Remove fish from heat and transfer to plates. Serve the aïoli on the side, and garnish with fresh sliced scallions.

Serves 4

Mocha Bean Cookies

½ cup butter, softened
½ cup brown sugar
¼ cup sugar
1 egg
1 teaspoon vanilla
1¼ cups flour
½ teaspoon baking soda
½ teaspoon salt
6 ounces chocolate mocha beans
½ cup chopped, toasted hazelnuts

Preheat oven to 350 degrees.

Cream butter and sugars together. Add egg and vanilla and mix well. Blend in dry ingredients, in 3 batches, until well mixed. Fold in mocha beans and chopped hazelnuts.

Drop tablespoons of dough onto greased cookie sheet. Bake 8 to 10 minutes or until golden brown. Serve warm or cooled.

143

Makes 4 dozen cookies

Pasta Lunch for 4

Barley Salad

Chicken Herb Tortelli with
Hazelnut Morel Sauce

Cherry Tart with Strawberries
and Dark Chocolate

Pasta is one of the tastiest, easiest, and most versatile meals you can make. It can be rich with egg yolk and cheese, or light, with just olive oil and fresh tomatoes. This lunch menu features a stuffed pasta—tortelli filled with chicken and fresh herbs—covered in a rich, creamy sauce full of meaty morel mushrooms and crunchy hazelnuts.

Lunch begins with a salad that uses barley, a grain overlooked by many cooks. Barley is a healthy addition to your diet, because it contains lots of fiber. It also has a wonderful texture, reminiscent of wild rice. I add barley to soups, toss it with dressing and add it to green salads, and mix it in tuna and chicken salad. As with many salads whose flavors are enhanced by sitting for a while, this one is better made the night before. The flavors really begin to marry and the barley is much tastier the next day.

To make the tortelli, I use ready-made sheets of fresh pasta, which you can find at Italian groceries or specialty food stores. Premade fresh pasta sheets save you a lot of time, but if you have the time you can make your pasta fresh. The sauce is made with true morels, but you can substitute the early spring morels or dried morels. If you use dried mushrooms, you will need only about one-third the amount of fresh ones.

For a true spring finish, I offer a tart filled with an interesting combination of dried cherries and red wine. These two ingredients give the filling a depth of flavor that is enhanced by mascarpone, a soft, rich Italian cream cheese. Topping this delicious mixture are the season's early strawberries and dark chocolate. Chocolate, cherries, and strawberries are a traditional dessert combination, but it's the addition of red wine that really brings out the earthy goodness of this great dessert.

Barley Salad

¼ cup barley
1 cup water
1 small red onion, diced medium
1 red pepper, diced medium
2 icicle radishes, thinly sliced
2 sprigs of rosemary, finely chopped
1 garlic clove, finely chopped
1 tablespoon Dijon mustard
1 tablespoon herb vinegar
2 tablespoons extra virgin olive oil
Salt and pepper to taste

In a small saucepan over high heat, bring barley and water to a boil, then lower heat and simmer until the water has evaporated. Stir barley and remove from stove to cool.

Place diced onion and pepper in a medium-size, stainless steel bowl. Mix in radishes, rosemary, and garlic. Add cooled barley and mix well.

146

In a separate bowl, stir together mustard and vinegar. Whisk in oil to emulsify. Season with salt and pepper. Add dressing to barley and mix well. Cover and refrigerate until used. Serve at room temperature.

Serves 4

Chicken Herb Tortelli
with Hazelnut Morel Sauce

Sauce

½ pound fresh morel mushrooms, coarsely chopped
*   (or 1 ounce dried morel mushrooms)*
¼ cup Frangelico hazelnut liqueur
2 shallots, finely chopped
1 garlic clove, finely chopped
¼ cup toasted, chopped hazelnuts
½ cup heavy cream
Salt and pepper to taste

Stuffed Pasta

4 ounces mild goat cheese
½ tablespoon assorted finely chopped herbs
*   (such as basil, thyme, oregano)*
2 boneless chicken breasts, skin removed
Salt and cracked black pepper to taste
2 sheets of premade flat pasta (approximately
*   9 inches by 11 inches each)*

1 teaspoon salt
Splash of olive oil

Chopped hazelnuts and fresh herb sprigs for garnish

To make the sauce: Place morels, Frangelico, shallots, and garlic in a medium-size saucepan over high heat. Reduce slightly and add hazelnuts and cream. Reduce again until sauce is thick and flavorful. Season with salt and pepper. Reserve.

To make the stuffed pasta: Place cheese, herbs, and seasonings in a small bowl and mix well. Place chicken in work bowl of a food processor fitted with the metal blade.

147

Process until chicken is finely ground. Add cheese mixture to chicken, season with salt and cracked pepper, and process again until well mixed.

Cut pasta sheets into 5-inch squares. Place a tablespoon of the cheese-chicken mixture in the middle of each square and fold over to form a 2½-inch-by-5-inch rectangle. Holding each end of the rectangle, twist slightly, to look somewhat like candy twists. Continue until all filling is used.

Fill a large pot with water; add salt and a splash of olive oil. Bring to a gentle boil. Drop tortellis in the water and cook about 3 to 4 minutes. Remove with a slotted spoon, drain, and distribute on plates.

Drizzle sauce over cooked pasta. Garnish with chopped hazelnuts and fresh herb sprigs.

Serves 4

NOTE: This makes about 4 very large tortellis per person. You can also make smaller squares, and serve them as appetizers. If you make appetizers for a large number of people, extend the filling by adding enough cream cheese to make it approximately one-third of the filling.

Cherry Tart with Strawberries and Dark Chocolate

Crust

2 cups flour
½ cup powdered sugar
½ teaspoon vanilla
Pinch of salt
1 cup unsalted butter

Filling

1 cup dry red wine
¾ cup sugar
1 cup dried Bing cherries
8 ounces mascarpone cheese

13 ounces bittersweet chocolate
2 pints strawberries, cleaned and hulled

To make the crust: Preheat oven to 350 degrees. Place all ingredients except butter in the bowl of a mixer or food processor. With the motor running, slowly add pieces of butter until dough forms a ball and pulls away from the sides of the bowl. Remove and press evenly onto bottom and sides of a greased flan pan. Bake until golden brown, about 10 minutes. Remove from oven, cool, and reserve.

To make the filling: In a medium-size saucepan, heat wine and sugar over high heat until liquid boils and sugar is dissolved. Add dried Bing cherries (Chukar brand) and cook until they are soft and plump. Cool. Blend cherry mixture in a food processor until it forms a smooth paste. Transfer to a mixing bowl and fold in mascarpone cheese. Pour into prebaked tart shell and refrigerate until set, about 25 to 30 minutes. Reserve.

To finish: Melt chocolate in a metal bowl set over boiling

water. Arrange whole strawberries, point end up, on top of the filling, spiraling around in concentric circles. When all the berries have been placed on top of the tart, drizzle with melted chocolate. Chill well. Let warm just slightly before cutting, so the chocolate doesn't crack.

Makes 1 tart

SPRING TEA FOR 6

Open-faced Spot Prawn Sandwiches with
Watercress and Cucumber Slices

Hazelnut Butter on Honey Wheat Toast

Smoked Chicken Sandwiches
with Spicy Honey Butter

Candied Ginger Scones

Orange and Almond Tartlets

Individual Angel Food Cakes
with Strawberry Compote

I CAN'T THINK OF A MORE PLEA-
surable way to celebrate the sun and spring than to serve tea
to a group of your best friends, on your deck or in a field of
wildflowers, using your nicest china. The White Rabbit and
the Mad Hatter will have nothing on you as you wile away a
few afternoon hours, leisurely eating open-faced sandwiches
and delicate sweets, and sipping tea.

This menu is a medley of tea sandwiches and sweets,
ranging in flavor from spicy to savory to sweet. Although
I describe only a couple of them here, all are special, highly
individualized tastes that add up to a kind of storybook
picnic.

One of the more exotic of these tastes is the chicken
sandwich, which pairs the rich flavor of smoked meat with a
sweet and spicy butter flavored with a Malaysian chile condi-
ment called *sambal oelek*. Sambal can usually be found at any
specialty food store or oriental grocery, but if you can't find
it, use any chile paste or dry ground cayenne pepper.

No tea would be complete without traditional English
scones. These have the exotic sweet and spicy flavors of
ground and crystallized ginger added. Most of the spreads
and desserts can be prepared well ahead of time.

To serve your guests, artfully arrange the sandwiches
and sweets on pretty platters and garnish with watercress
and colorful edible flowers, such as pansies, violas, or calendulas. Present them to your guests on your deck or patio, or
on a picnic blanket in a lovely park. Serve a variety of
refreshing teas, from herbal to Chinese green. Then relax and
savor spring's fancies.

Open-faced Spot Prawn Sandwiches with Watercress and Cucumber Slices

6 to 8 large spot prawns, peeled
1 tablespoon olive oil
6 slices egg bread
¼ cup butter, softened
1 English cucumber, peeled and thinly sliced
1 bunch fresh watercress, washed

Sauté prawns in olive oil over high heat just until they turn pink. Cool and cut in half lengthwise. Toast bread, cut into rectangles (about 4 inches by 1½ inches), and spread with butter. Place a cucumber slice on each slice, then half a prawn, and top with a sprig of watercress. Cover with plastic wrap and chill until ready to serve.

Makes about 18 rectangles

VARIATIONS: Instead of watercress, use other fresh herbs, such as tarragon, cilantro, or sorrel. Also try other types of breads to change the sandwiches.

153

Hazelnut Butter on Honey Wheat Toast

½ cup toasted hazelnuts
2 teaspoons sugar
1 tablespoon Frangelico hazelnut liqueur
1 cup butter
6 slices good-quality honey wheat bread

Chop the nuts in a food processor. While the machine is running, add sugar and liqueur and continue processing until well mixed. Again, while the machine is running, slowly add butter until incorporated. Reserve.

Toast bread, then cut each piece into 4 triangles. Spread hazelnut butter onto the toast triangles and refrigerate (covered) until ready to serve.

Makes about 24 triangles

HINT: If you have any hazelnut butter left over, freeze it to use later on french toast or pancakes.

VARIATIONS: You can make this butter with any other nuts, such as almonds or pecans.

Smoked Chicken Sandwiches
with Spicy Honey Butter

1 bunch scallions, diced
1 tablespoon honey
1 teaspoon finely chopped cilantro
½ teaspoon sambal oelek
1 cup butter, softened
1 smoked chicken breast, skin removed and thinly sliced
6 slices molasses bread

Cilantro for garnish

Place scallions, honey, cilantro, and sambal oelek into a
mixing bowl or food processor. Process until onions are finely
ground. Add butter and process until well mixed. Store in the
refrigerator if not using right away.

Cut molasses bread into rounds using a 2-inch round
cookie cutter. Toast bread rounds. Spread honey butter on
toasted rounds, top with chicken slices, and garnish with a
cilantro leaf.

Serves 6

VARIATIONS: Try adding ½ teaspoon chopped gingerroot to
the butter or a teaspoon of Japanese wasabi paste. If you don't
care for spicy food, leave out the sambal oelek.

155

Candied Ginger Scones

3 cups flour
½ teaspoon baking soda
2 teaspoons cream of tartar
½ teaspoon ground ginger
½ cup butter, softened
1 tablespoon sugar
¼ cup milk
¼ cup water
2 tablespoons coarsely chopped candied ginger
1 egg, beaten

Preheat oven to 400 degrees.

Place flour, baking soda, cream of tartar, and ground ginger into a large mixing bowl. Work in butter until the mixture has a fine meal consistency. Blend in sugar. Combine milk and water and add to flour mixture to form a soft dough. Work in candied ginger.

Knead lightly and shape dough into a 10-inch-by-8-inch rectangle on a floured surface. Cut into 1-inch-by-3-inch triangles. Brush the tops with beaten egg. Bake 20 minutes or until lightly browned.

Makes 1 dozen scones

VARIATIONS: Try candied citrus peel instead of candied ginger. You can make savory scones, instead of sweet, by leaving out the sugar and adding ¼ cup lightly sautéed, chopped shallots, or 6 Oven Roasted Shallots (see page 229), and fresh chopped herbs, such as thyme or basil.

Orange and Almond Tartlets

Crust

¼ cup powdered sugar

½ cup unsalted butter

½ teaspoon vanilla

Pinch of salt

1 cup flour

Filling

¾ cup heavy cream

¼ cup almond paste

2 tablespoons sugar

½ cup ground toasted almonds

2 eggs

1 tablespoon Amaretto

6 round orange slices

Preheat oven to 350 degrees.

To make the crust: Cream together sugar and butter in a mixing bowl. Add vanilla and salt and mix well. Add flour and blend until the dough comes together. Press into bottom and sides of 6 greased tartlet pans. Bake 5 to 7 minutes. Cool.

To make the filling: In a medium-size mixing bowl combine cream, almond paste, sugar, and nuts. Blend well. Add eggs one at a time, mixing after each one. Mix in Amaretto.

Pour the filling into prebaked shells and top each tartlet with an orange slice. Bake at 350 degrees for about 15 minutes, or until a knife inserted comes clean. Remove from the oven and serve warm.

Makes 6 tartlets

Individual Angel Food Cakes
with Strawberry Compote

Cakes

1 tablespoon melted butter

1¼ cups sugar

6 egg whites

½ cup flour

½ teaspoon vanilla

1 teaspoon lemon zest

Compote

2 tablespoons butter

1 pint strawberries, washed, hulled, and quartered

¼ cup Simple Syrup (see page 230)

1 tablespoon Crème de Cassis (black currant liqueur)

1 teaspoon chopped fresh mint

Preheat oven to 350 degrees.

To make the cakes: Brush 6 6-ounce ramekins with butter, then coat with ¼ cup sugar and reserve.

In a clean mixing bowl, whip egg whites on high speed until foamy. Slowly add 1 cup sugar and continue whipping until the whites are stiff but not dry. Gently fold in half the flour, then the other half. When the flour is incorporated, fold in the vanilla and lemon zest. Divide batter among the ramekins, tapping each one gently to force out any air pockets.

Bake about 15 minutes, until cakes are golden brown and spring back when touched in the middle. Remove from oven, let stand 5 minutes, then flip over and cool upside down.

To make the compote: In a large heavy sauté pan over high heat, melt butter and add the strawberries. Cook berries until heated. Add Simple Syrup and Crème de Cassis and bring to a boil. Remove from heat. Add mint. Remove cakes from baking dishes and serve with hot or cold compote.

Makes 6 cakes

VARIATIONS: Try making the compote with other fresh berries, such as blackberries or huckleberries. Other liqueurs may be used instead of Crème de Cassis, such as Grand Marnier or Chambord.

CRAB FRITTATA BREAKFAST FOR 4

Crab Frittata

Lemon Verbena Bread

Scalloped Potatoes with Horseradish
and Herb Cheese

A SUNNY MORNING CAN GET ANY-
one up and going. After a breakfast like this, I can even con-
vince myself that weeding our huge yard is not a chore but
an exciting challenge (though I'm not optimistic enough to
say a "joy").

This is a very casual breakfast, one that I would just lay
out buffet-style. It features a frittata, which is like an
omelette, but open faced, with the ingredients mixed with the
eggs rather than stuffed in the middle with the eggs folded
over. Frittatas are easy and quite versatile. You can add seasonal vegetables, shrimp, or good-quality smoked ham slices.

The key to making a good frittata is having all your
ingredients ready to go, which in the cooking trade is called
mise en place. It's a French phrase that means "everything in
its place," and it is a concept that is the key to timing when
preparing a great meal. When I was in cooking school, I
remember many mornings, sitting in class at 7:00 A.M., hearing *mise en place* repeated over and over by the instructors.
They never let us forget the importance of being prepared.

The quick bread in this breakfast contains one of my
favorite herbs, lemon verbena—which, as its name implies,
has a fragrant lemon smell. It may be hard for you to find in
a local market; the best way to be sure it's available is grow it
yourself. In our herb garden, it grows like a weed all summer
long. I dry it in order to have some on hand all winter.

Potatoes are one of my favorite forms of carbohydrate.
These breakfast potatoes have the bite of fresh horseradish,
combined with the creamy consistency of herb cheese and
heavy cream. They make great leftovers—that is, if there are
any left. With my family, a potato dish is never safe.

Crab Frittata

12 large eggs
½ cup milk
1 teaspoon chopped fresh lemon thyme
Salt and pepper to taste
3 tablespoons unsalted butter
2 shallots, finely chopped
3 garlic cloves, finely chopped
1 small onion, diced small
1 small zucchini, julienned
1 small carrot, julienned
1 small yellow squash, julienned
1 cup sliced domestic mushrooms
1 cup crabmeat
¼ cup grated Parmesan cheese
Lemon wedges for garnish

Crack eggs into a medium-size bowl and add milk, lemon thyme, and salt and pepper. Whisk in the milk and break up the yolks. Set aside.

In a very large, ovenproof sauté pan (about 12 to 14 inches), heat butter until melted. Add shallots and garlic, and sauté over high heat until you can smell the aroma. Add onion and sauté until tender. Add vegetables and sauté until *al dente* or tender. Add crabmeat and mix well. Pour eggs into the vegetables and crabmeat and stir with a fork to mix.

Continue cooking over high heat, constantly stirring with the fork until the eggs just start to set. Move to oven, and continue cooking on the first rack under the broiler, just until the eggs set, about 3 to 4 minutes. Remove from oven and slice into quarters. Sprinkle grated Parmesan cheese on top and garnish with fresh lemon wedges.

Serves 4

Lemon Verbena Bread

2⅓ cups flour
1½ teaspoons baking powder
½ teaspoon salt
1½ cups sugar
¾ cup butter, softened
3 large eggs
½ cup buttermilk
½ cup sour cream
1 tablespoon lemon zest
2 teaspoons finely chopped lemon verbena

Glaze
2 tablespoons sugar
Juice of 1 lemon

Preheat oven to 350 degrees.

In a large bowl, combine flour, baking powder, salt, and sugar. Add softened butter and mix with a fork until flour mixture resembles coarse crumbs. In a medium-size mixing bowl, mix together eggs, butter, milk, sour cream, lemon zest, and lemon verbena. Add to flour mixture and mix just until batter comes together. Pour batter into a greased and floured 9-inch-by-5-inch loaf pan and bake about 1½ hours, or until a knife inserted comes out clean.

In a small mixing bowl blend together sugar and lemon juice. Once the loaf is pulled from the oven, prick top with a fork. Then brush on glaze, a little at a time, as the bread cools, until all the glaze has been used. Serve warm or cold.

Makes 1 loaf

NOTE: This bread freezes well. Just warm it a bit before serving to bring out the lemon flavors.

163

Scalloped Potatoes with Horseradish and Herb Cheese

4 large potatoes
1 teaspoon grated fresh horseradish
1 cup heavy cream
4 ounces herbed double-cream cheese (Boursin)
1 medium onion, thinly sliced
½ cup grated Parmesan cheese
Salt and cracked black pepper

Preheat oven to 350 degrees.

Slice the potatoes very thin and store in a bowl of water until needed. In a small bowl combine horseradish, cream, and herb cheese. Mix well.

Liberally butter a 9-inch baking pan. Place a layer of potatoes on the bottom, then a layer of onion. Sprinkle with Parmesan cheese, then layer again with potatoes, onions, and cheese. Repeat until all the potatoes and onions are used. Pour cream mixture over everything and top with the last of the Parmesan cheese.

Bake 45 minutes to 1 hour, or until potatoes are tender and cheese is golden brown. Let sit 5 minutes before cutting to allow it to set up a bit.

Serves 4

Spring Scrambled Eggs for 6

Minted Melon

Herbed Pork Patties

Scrambled Eggs with Pancetta
and Early Spring Morels

Yogurt Bran Muffins

I'M NOT EXACTLY WHAT YOU WOULD consider a "morning person." In fact, people tend to steer clear of me at least until after I've had my first cup of coffee. So if I am going to get up really early, there has to be a special reason. This breakfast is it. It can be served course by course or buffet style. I prefer the latter because I think breakfast should be casual and relaxed. The melons can be prepared the night before, then dished into chilled glasses just before breakfast. Likewise, the pork patties can be prepared the night before then fried in the morning.

The pork patties are made with tenderloin combined with fatback and herbs. The fatback adds just the right amount of fat so that the meat does not become dry and tasteless. While we should steer clear of fat as much as possible, a tasty sausage depends on fat, so make this an exception.

Scrambled eggs are made at the last moment before serving breakfast. You can have everything cut and ready to go, however. Remember—*mise en place.* Italian pancetta ham adds a peppery flavor to these eggs, and the early morels a smokiness. If early spring morels are unavailable, either fresh or dried true morels are a good substitute. The difference is that early spring morels are not as rich and smoky as true morels. Also the stem and cap are two distinct pieces in early springs, whereas they are one continuous piece in true morels. Scrambled eggs should be cooked quickly, but not overcooked until dry; they should be soft, but not runny. If you add cheese, be sure to add it just before the eggs are finished. Allow them to cook just until the cheese has started to melt.

Yogurt gives the muffins extra tang and moistness, while the bran flakes and orange zest give them a distinctive texture. These muffins are especially delicious served warm, with different flavored butters—such as orange, spiced honey, or mint.

Minted Melon

2 cantaloupes, split and cleaned of seeds
2 honeydew melons, split and cleaned of seeds
1 cup champagne
¼ cup sugar
2 teaspoons chopped mint

6 mint sprigs for garnish

Scoop melon into balls with a melon scoop and place in a medium-size bowl. Combine champagne, sugar, and chopped mint in a small saucepan and bring to a boil over high heat. Pour over melon and cool in the refrigerator.

Serve in frosted glasses and garnish with fresh mint sprigs.

Serves 6

NOTE: If you don't have a melon scoop, you can remove the rind, cut in half, and slice into thin slices.

VARIATIONS: Use other flavors instead of mint, such as rose geranium or orange mint. You can also substitute other wines, such as port or Riesling, for the champagne. Both wines are a nice complement to mint.

Herbed Pork Patties

¼ pound pork fatback, cut in large cubes
1½ pounds pork tenderloin, cut in large cubes
1 small onion, finely diced
3 garlic cloves, finely chopped
1 tablespoon finely chopped fresh thyme
Salt and pepper to taste
1 tablespoon vegetable oil

In a food processor, finely grind the cubed fatback and pork together, stopping frequently to scrape down the sides. Transfer the ground meat to a medium-size mixing bowl and add onion, garlic, thyme, and salt and pepper. Mix well and shape into 6 patties.

In a large sauté pan, heat the oil over high heat. Place patties in the pan and cook until well browned. Remove from pan and drain any oil. Keep warm until ready to serve.

Serves 6

Scrambled Eggs with Pancetta and Early Spring Morels

2 tablespoons unsalted butter
⅓ pound pancetta, diced into small cubes
3 shallots, finely chopped
2 garlic cloves, finely chopped
½ pound early spring morel mushrooms, coarsely chopped
12 eggs, slightly beaten
Salt and pepper to taste

Heat butter in a large sauté pan and add the diced pancetta. Cook over medium-high heat until crisp. Add chopped shallots, garlic, and morels. Sauté slightly just until you smell the aroma. Add beaten eggs and mix well. Cook eggs to a soft consistency (do not overcook or the eggs will become dry). Season to taste.

Serves 6

NOTE: The scrambled eggs should be made at the last moment so they don't dry out.

VARIATIONS: Try using other wild mushrooms, such as chanterelles or oyster mushrooms.

Yogurt Bran Muffins

3 cups bran flakes
1¼ cups flour
½ cup sugar
1¼ teaspoon baking soda
¼ teaspoon salt
1 teaspoon orange zest
1 large egg
¾ cup yogurt
¼ cup milk
¼ cup vegetable oil

Preheat oven to 400 degrees.

Combine dry ingredients in a large mixing bowl. Add egg, yogurt, milk, and oil, and stir until just mixed. Spoon batter into greased and floured muffin tins. Bake 25 to 30 minutes.

Leave the muffins in the pan to cool for 5 minutes before removing and serving. (It is a good idea to loosen the muffins slightly before you let them cool.)

Makes 1 dozen muffins

VARIATIONS: Try adding lemon zest to these muffins. Other nice variations are to add ½ teaspoon cinnamon and/or other spices, such as nutmeg, ginger, or cardamom.

SUMMER

Seared Tuna Dinner for 4

Whole Roasted Garlic
with Herb Mustard and Croutons

Grilled Corn Soup with
Red Pepper Crème Fraîche

Seared Tuna with Jalapeño Lime Mayonnaise

White Chocolate Raspberry Almond Torte

Wine Suggestion
Sokol Blosser "Redland" Pinot Noir

Among the best things that summer has to offer are two of my favorite fresh ingredients—corn and raspberries. When the first local corn arrives in the markets, I feel like summer has finally arrived. The pungent, homemade herb mustard that accompanies the Roasted Garlic and Croutons, this dinner's appetizer, is not only a delicious member of this trio, it makes a great Christmas gift. If you decide to try it, make a double batch and put some up for presents.

Local corn first arrives in Northwest markets in July. At my house, we prepare corn a lot of different ways, from fried to grilled. We often grill it right on the barbecue (removing the silk but keeping the husks on). The corn soup recipe uses grilled corn—with the husks removed—to give the soup a rich smoky flavor. Buy corn that is as freshly picked as possible, because the longer corn sits, the more its natural sugars convert to starch. Look for corn that has no apparent mold spots or rotting or dried kernels, and a firm moist husk.

The entree features fresh ahi, or yellowfin tuna. Try to obtain a sushi or import grade tuna to assure that you are getting the best and freshest tuna available. If tuna is impossible to find in your area, swordfish or sturgeon are equally good. I prefer my tuna medium rare to rare, when the texture reminds me of a very high-quality beef tenderloin. The longer you cook tuna, the drier and oilier it becomes, until it eventually resembles canned tuna. Try medium rare; if it doesn't appeal to you, put it back on the stove and cook it a little longer.

Although I love desserts, I'm not a great fan of supersweet ones. I like them sweet, with a tart bite at the end. Raspberries and chocolate have that nice contrast. Don't be fooled by all the steps in the torte recipe; it is really very simple to make. Although you can make this torte ahead, don't make it any earlier than the morning of your dinner, because raspberries are delicate and don't hold up long.

Whole Roasted Garlic with Herb Mustard and Croutons

Mustard

½ cup light mustard seeds

3 tablespoons dry mustard

⅔ cup water

¾ cup white wine vinegar or herb vinegar

2 garlic cloves, finely chopped

1 teaspoon sugar

2 teaspoons salt

2 tablespoons chopped mixed fresh herbs
        (tarragon, thyme, and marjoram)

Croutons

1 loaf day-old french bread

3 tablespoons olive oil

2 large bulbs Roasted Garlic (see page 229)

Small round of mild goat cheese (optional)

Fresh greens and edible flowers for garnish

To make the mustard: Place mustard seeds, dry mustard, and water in a medium-size bowl and mix well. Let sit 2 hours at room temperature. Stir the mixture every 10 to 15 minutes. Place mustard mixture in a food processor or blender and grind to desired consistency; longer for a smooth consistency and shorter for a coarser ground mustard. Add all remaining ingredients and blend completely.

Spoon mustard into clean lidded jars and store at room temperature until it mellows. It will be very hot at first. I usually store mine about a month, checking from time to time to see how it is progressing. Once the mustard is as mellow as you want it, transfer to the refrigerator to store. Mustard will keep several months in the refrigerator.

Makes 2 cups.

To make the croutons: Preheat oven to 350 degrees. Slice the bread thin and place on a small sheet pan. Brush the slices with olive oil and brown in oven.

To serve: Arrange Roasted Garlic and croutons on a medium-size serving plate. If you like, put out a mild, soft goat cheese. Garnish with fresh greens and edible flowers. Serve the homemade mustard on the side in a small crock.

Serves 4

NOTE: If you want to put up some mustard for Christmas presents, use home canning jars and lids. Seal the jars in a boiling water bath.

175

Grilled Corn Soup with
Red Pepper Crème Fraîche

Red Pepper Crème Fraîche
1 red bell pepper
1 cup Crème Fraîche (see page 230)
Salt and pepper to taste

Soup
8 ears fresh corn, silk and husks removed
2 tablespoons unsalted butter
1 medium yellow onion, diced small
2 garlic cloves, finely chopped
4 shallots, finely chopped
1 pint strong Chicken Stock (see page 227)
2 cups heavy cream
Salt and pepper to taste

Sprigs of fresh greens for garnish

To make the red pepper Crème Fraîche: Roast red pepper under a broiler (about 4 inches) until the skin is evenly blackened and blistered. Cover with a towel and cool. Remove skin (it will slip off easily), remove all the seeds and stems, and puree. Add pepper puree to the Crème Fraîche and season with salt and pepper. Refrigerate until ready to serve.

To make the soup: On a grill or barbecue, place corn on grill set about 6 inches over hot, glowing coals. Cook corn about 7 to 10 minutes, turning occasionally to ensure that kernels are evenly grilled. Remove from heat and cut corn off the cob. Reserve.

Heat butter in a large saucepan over high heat. Add onion, garlic, and shallots, and sauté until you begin to smell the aroma. Add corn and sauté about 2 to 3 minutes. Pour in Chicken Stock, reduce heat to medium, and simmer

5 minutes. Remove soup from heat and puree in a blender
or food processor. Return mixture to pan, add cream, and
simmer on medium heat until thick. Season with salt and
pepper.

To serve soup, pour into bowls, swirl in red pepper
Crème Fraîche, and garnish with a sprig of fresh greens.
This soup can be served hot or cold.

Serves 4

NOTES: For a Southwestern touch, finish the soup with
1 teaspoon of chopped cilantro and cayenne to taste. If your
soup becomes too thick, thin it with Chicken Stock or milk.

Seared Tuna with Jalapeño Lime Mayonnaise

Mayonnaise

¼ cup rice wine vinegar
Juice of 1 lime
1 tablespoon Dijon mustard
3 shallots, finely chopped
2 garlic cloves, finely chopped
1 tablespoon finely chopped, pickled jalapeño peppers
2 egg yolks
1 cup vegetable oil
Salt and pepper to taste

2 tablespoons vegetable oil
4 7-ounce ahi tuna fillets
1 teaspoon hot chile flakes
Salt and pepper to taste

Lime zest and whole red jalapeño peppers for garnish

To make the mayonnaise: In a medium-size mixing bowl, combine vinegar, lime juice, mustard, shallots, garlic, jalapeños, and egg yolks and mix well. Slowly whisk in salad oil to emulsify. Season with salt and pepper. Refrigerate in a covered jar until ready to use.

To sear the tuna: Heat a large sauté pan with 1 tablespoon vegetable oil until smoking hot. Brush the other tablespoon of oil on the tuna fillets. Season fillets on both sides with the chile flakes, salt, and pepper. Place tuna in the hot pan and cook to medium rare, about 2 minutes on each side.

Transfer tuna to plate and serve mayonnaise on top or on the side. Garnish with lime zest and whole red jalapeños.

Serves 4

White Chocolate Raspberry Almond Torte

Torte
½ pound white chocolate
½ pound unsalted butter
1 cup almond paste
6 large eggs
2 cups toasted ground almonds
⅓ cup Amaretto

Topping
3 ounces bittersweet chocolate
1 tablespoon unsalted butter
2 pints raspberries, cleaned
2 ounces white chocolate

To make the torte: Preheat oven to 350 degrees. Fill a large roasting pan with about ¼ inch of water and place in oven.

Melt white chocolate and butter in a medium-size metal bowl set over, but not touching, boiling water. While chocolate is melting, soften almond paste in a bowl using a mixer on medium speed. Lower mixing speed and add eggs. Mix 2 minutes. Slowly add melted white chocolate while on slow speed, then add almonds and Amaretto and mix a few minutes more.

When all ingredients are thoroughly blended, place the batter in a 9-inch cake pan, greased, lightly floured, and lined on the bottom with parchment paper. Set the cake pan in the oven water bath and bake 25 to 30 minutes, or until a knife inserted comes out clean.

Cool 5 minutes and remove from cake pan. Let the torte cool while making the topping.

To make the topping: Melt dark chocolate and butter in a small metal bowl set over, but not touching, boiling water.

Once the chocolate mixture has melted, cool slightly to thicken. Spread evenly on the top of the torte.

Before the chocolate cools completely, set raspberries on top of the torte, beginning in the middle and spiraling around in a circular fashion until the torte is covered.

Once the raspberries are on the torte, melt the white chocolate in a metal bowl set over (not touching) boiling water (be sure to melt it very slowly or it will lump up). Spoon melted white chocolate into a pastry bag fitted with a small plain tube. Drizzle the chocolate over the torte to form a lacy pattern. Refrigerate until ready to serve.

Makes 1 9-inch torte

VARIATIONS: This torte can be made with just about any berry. I have used marionberries, blackberries, and strawberries.

PEPPERED BEEF TENDERLOIN DINNER
FOR 6

Warmed Greens with
Hazelnut Tarragon Dressing

Peppered Beef Tenderloin
with Cherry Hollandaise

Blackberry Crème Caramel

WINE SUGGESTION
Leonetti Cabernet Sauvignon

FOR A SUMMER EVENING, THIS IS the perfect menu. It is simple, has great textures and flavors, and a lot of it can be made ahead, which is especially gratifying at the end of a warm day.

The wild or field greens that go into the salad are a mix of baby lettuces, flowers, and herbs that add a pleasing complexity. The flavors are balanced so that you don't get only strong or bitter flavors. These greens may be expensive, so you can mix in some leaf lettuce to stretch them a bit if you wish.

A nice balance of textures and flavors is also found in the beef tenderloin. I have added cherries cooked in red wine to traditional hollandaise to add a rich, sweet flavor to complement the beef. Hollandaise is usually tart or savory. My variation on this sauce is typical of my approach to cooking. I like to take classic ideas and find interesting ways to vary them.

In the Northwest, cherries come into the markets around the beginning or the middle of May, depending on the weather. I like Bing cherries because they have a deep cherry flavor, but are not overly sweet. Select firm cherries that are ripe but not over-ripe, or the sauce will be too sweet.

Vegetables such as boiled new potatoes tossed with a balsamic vinaigrette, or steamed asparagus with Crème Fraîche flavored with orange zest would make a wonderful side dish for this tenderloin.

Another new twist on a classic recipe—adding pureed blackberries to custard to create Blackberry Crème Caramel. Nothing can beat a fresh blackberry dessert, and from the end of July into August, you should be able to pick berries fresh or find them in local markets.

Warmed Greens with Hazelnut Tarragon Dressing

Dressing
¼ cup white wine vinegar or tarragon vinegar
2 tablespoons Dijon mustard
2 shallots, finely chopped
2 garlic cloves, finely chopped
1 tablespoon finely chopped fresh tarragon
    or ½ tablespoon dried tarragon
1 egg yolk
⅓ cup hazelnut oil
½ cup vegetable oil

Greens
½ pound wild local greens
¼ pound oyster mushrooms, sliced
½ cup toasted chopped hazelnuts
3 Roma tomatoes, quartered

½ cup grated imported Romano or Parmesan cheese

To make the dressing: Mix vinegar, mustard, shallots, garlic, tarragon, and egg yolk in a medium-size metal bowl. Slowly whisk in oils one at a time, making sure the mixture is emulsifying. Season to taste with salt and pepper.

To prepare the salad: In a large metal bowl place greens, mushrooms, hazelnuts, and tomatoes. In a heavy sauté pan, heat ¾ cup of dressing just to a boil. Pour over the greens and toss.

Distribute on individual salad plates and sprinkle with grated cheese.

Serves 6

Peppered Beef Tenderloin with Cherry Hollandaise

Hollandaise

1 cup dry red wine
⅓ cup red wine vinegar
2 shallots, finely chopped
3 garlic cloves, finely chopped
1 cup pitted, chopped Bing cherries
4 egg yolks
1¼ cups unsalted butter, melted
Salt and pepper to taste

Tenderloins

2 tablespoons vegetable oil
6 5-ounce beef tenderloins
6 tablespoons cracked black pepper
Salt to taste

Fresh cherries and watercress sprigs for garnish

To make the hollandaise: In a heavy saucepan over high heat, combine wine, vinegar, shallots, garlic, and cherries and reduce by half. Place egg yolks in a medium-size metal bowl and whisk just enough to break apart. Temper the yolks with the reduced liquid to bring them to the same temperature. Stir the rest of the reduced mixture into the yolks.

Place the bowl of yolks over a pan of boiling water and cook, whisking constantly, until the mixture is thick and foamy (like soft whipped cream). Remove bowl from the heat and slowly whisk in the melted butter. Season with salt and pepper. Set bowl in a water bath to keep warm, but not hot.

To prepare the beef tenderloin: Preheat oven to 375 degrees. In a heavy, ovenproof sauté pan, heat oil until smoking hot. While oil is heating, press 1 tablespoon of cracked black pepper onto each tenderloin and season with salt. Quickly sear both sides of the tenderloins in the hot pan. Transfer to oven and finish to desired doneness (about 10 minutes for medium to medium rare).

Transfer to plates and sauce each tenderloin with about 2 ounces of hollandaise. Garnish with fresh cherries and a sprig of watercress.

Serves 6

NOTE: If your hollandaise separates, add 2 tablespoons of cold water and whisk well, or place 1 egg yolk in a medium-size metal bowl and slowly whisk in the broken hollandaise.

Blackberry Crème Caramel

1 cup sugar
¼ cup water
2 cups half-and-half
¾ cup blackberry puree, strained (about 2 pints whole
    blackberries)
½ cup sugar
½ teaspoon vanilla
5 large eggs, slightly beaten

Fresh blackberries and mint sprigs for garnish

Lightly grease 6 6-ounce ramekins. Preheat oven to 350 degrees. Fill large roasting pan with about ¼ inch of water and set in oven.

Place sugar and water in a small heavy sauté pan and cook over high heat until the sugar turns light brown. While the sugar is caramelizing, do not stir. If small crystals begin to form on the sides of the pan, wash them with a pastry brush and cold water. Once the caramel is light brown, distribute equal amounts in the bottom of each ramekin. Cool.

Stir together half-and-half, blackberry puree, sugar, and vanilla in a medium-size mixing bowl until well mixed. Add beaten eggs and mix. Pour about ½ cup of custard mix in each ramekin.

Set the ramekins in the water bath and bake 40 to 50 minutes, or until a knife inserted comes out clean. Remove from water bath and refrigerate 2 hours. When ready to serve, run a warm knife around the inside of each ramekin and flip the crème caramel onto a dessert plate. Garnish with fresh blackberries and mint.

Serves 6

THE FIRST SUMMER BARBECUE FOR 4

Cucumber Salad with Ginger
and Rice Wine Vinegar

Warm Potato Salad with Lemon Verbena Dressing

Whole Roasted Chicken with Spicy Glaze

Caramelized Peach Flan

WINE SUGGESTION
Hogue Reserve Merlot

Roasting a chicken whole on the grill is my favorite way to cook it. The skin crisps beautifully and the meat inside is tender and juicy. This barbecue menu features grilled chicken with a spicy glaze with a sweet and hot Oriental flavor.

To grill chicken successfully, make sure your coals are not too hot (you should be able to hold your hand just over the grill for about 2 seconds) and the chicken is placed at a proper distance from them—about 6 inches. Otherwise the skin will be burned and the meat raw. You can also precook the chicken 15 to 20 minutes at 350 degrees in the oven, then finish it on the grill, or cut it into pieces instead of grilling whole.

The chicken follows two light and refreshing salads, cucumber and potato. The cucumber is crisp and tangy, with tones of ginger, while the potato salad is warm, with citrus flavors and a light vinaigrette dressing.

For dessert, rich ripe peaches are cooked with caramelized sugar in a buttery crust. Be careful when cooking the tart that you don't overcook and allow the peaches to get mushy. You can also substitute nectarines and apricots for the peaches in this tart.

Cucumber Salad with Ginger and Rice Wine Vinegar

2 English cucumbers, sliced paper thin
1 cup rice wine vinegar
1 tablespoon sugar
2 teaspoons grated gingerroot
Salt and pepper to taste

Place thinly sliced cucumbers in a medium-size bowl. In a small bowl or mixing cup, mix together vinegar, sugar, and ginger, and season with salt and pepper. Pour over cucumbers and toss. Adjust seasonings and let stand (unrefrigerated), in a covered bowl, for 1 hour. Serve at room temperature.

Serves 4

VARIATIONS: You can spice up this salad with a bit of sambal oelek or chile flakes. You might also try adding some chopped fresh cilantro. I suggest you buy plain—not seasoned—rice wine vinegar; the seasoned variety tends to be too sweet.

189

Warm Potato Salad
with Lemon Verbena Dressing

1½ pounds new white potatoes, scrubbed (unpeeled)
3 shallots, finely chopped
3 garlic cloves, finely chopped
¼ cup champagne vinegar
¾ cup vegetable oil
1 tablespoon chopped fresh lemon verbena
Salt and pepper to taste

Boil whole potatoes in a large stockpot until tender when pricked with a fork. Drain and quarter potatoes and place in a medium-size bowl. In a separate mixing bowl, combine shallots, garlic, and vinegar. Slowly whisk in oil to emulsify. Mix in lemon verbena and season with salt and pepper. Toss dressing with warm potatoes and serve.

Serves 4

190

HINT: Try using different flavored vinegar and oils in this dressing. This salad also can be served cold and the dressing made several days ahead.

Whole Roasted Chicken with Spicy Glaze

2 2-pound roasting chickens
Salt and pepper to taste

Glaze
2 garlic cloves, finely chopped
2 shallots, finely chopped
1 teaspoon finely chopped gingerroot
2 tablespoons rice wine vinegar
1 tablespoon honey
2 tablespoons soy sauce
½ cup vegetable oil
1 teaspoon sambal oelek

Preheat oven to 425 degrees.

To precook the chickens: Arrange chickens in a large roasting pan so that they are not touching. Season with salt and pepper. Roast about 15 minutes in the oven, then transfer them to the grill, set about 6 inches over hot (not flaming) coals.

To make the glaze: In a medium-size bowl, combine all glaze ingredients and mix well. This glaze keeps in the refrigerator up to 2 weeks.

Once the chicken is on the grill, baste with glaze using a pastry brush. Baste about every 10 minutes until the chicken is done, about 45 minutes to 1 hour. You can tell when the chicken is done by piercing it in the wing joint. If the juices run clean, the chicken is done. If the juices contain blood, the chicken needs to cook longer.

Serves 4

VARIATIONS: Try this glaze on everything from pork tenderloins to ahi tuna.

Caramelized Peach Flan

Crust

1¼ cups flour
½ teaspoon salt
½ teaspoon cinnamon
¼ teaspoon ground ginger
½ cup butter
6 tablespoons cold water

Filling

6 large ripe peaches
½ cup water
½ cup sugar

Soft whipped cream

Preheat oven to 350 degrees.

To make the dough: Combine flour, salt, cinnamon, and ginger in a medium-size mixing bowl and stir. Cut butter into small pieces and cut into the flour mixture to form small bead-size pieces. Add cold water and stir just to combine. Wrap dough in plastic and refrigerate for 30 minutes.

Generously flour a cutting board, then roll dough to about ¼ inch thick. Press loosely onto bottom and sides of a greased 12-inch flan pan. Bake for 10 minutes. Remove from oven and cool.

To make the filling: Peel peaches and slice thin. Arrange sliced peaches in the flan shell in a circular fashion. In a small saucepan, combine sugar and water. Bring to a boil and cook until golden brown. Pour caramelized sugar over the peaches. Bake about 20 minutes, until peaches are tender. Serve warm with soft whipped cream.

Makes 1 12-inch flan

Summer Picnic for 4

Chilled Rice Salad with Sherry Vinaigrette

Marinated Oranges and Strawberries in
Grand Marnier and Black Pepper

Sweet Onion Herb Flan

John's Cured Broiled Salmon

Chocolate Chocolate-Chip Cheesecake Tart

BY A QUIET STREAM IN THE
mountains or in your living room by the fireplace on a drizzly day, casual or elegant and romantic, peanut butter and jelly sandwiches in a rucksack or roast pheasant in a classic wicker hamper—picnics are one of the most enjoyable ways to dine. This menu is designed for any kind of picnic—whether you take it to the beach or eat in your own back yard.

One of my favorite dishes in this menu is based on an idea from my friend Michael. It's a flan with sweet Walla Walla onions, fresh herbs, and goat cheese. Northwesterners always eagerly await Walla Walla onion season. These onions are so sweet, many people like to just eat them raw, like apples. When I was a child, visiting my grandparents in Pasco, Washington, Walla Wallas were plentiful and we ate lots of peanut butter and onion sandwiches. This flan is a more sophisticated tribute to these Northwest gems.

The centerpiece for this picnic is a crispy broiled salmon that begins with my husband John's once-secret cure recipe. The cure mix draws moisture from the salmon and if left on long enough, the fish will actually "cook," like gravlax or ceviche. The longer you leave the fish in the cure, the stronger the flavors will be. This recipe uses the curing technique to add flavor and draw some moisture out of the fish, but then the mix is rinsed off just before broiling. The salmon retains enough moisture so it isn't dry, and the sugar from the cure gives the fish a delicious crispiness.

The best thing about a picnic is how all the food looks spread before you. This picnic has a beautiful blend of flavors, textures, and colors. The rich red salmon is surrounded by tarts of onion and chocolate, a dish of colorful rice salad, and luscious marinated oranges and strawberries. The only trouble you'll have is deciding what to eat first.

Chilled Rice Salad with Sherry Vinaigrette

Vinaigrette

¼ cup sherry wine vinegar

2 tablespoons whole-grain mustard

2 garlic cloves, finely chopped

2 shallots, finely chopped

¼ cup dry sherry

⅓ cup extra virgin olive oil

⅔ cup vegetable oil

Salt and pepper to taste

1 bunch opal basil, finely chopped

Salad

2 cups cooked long-grain rice

1 red bell pepper, julienned

1 bunch scallions, cut diagonally (use a mix of the green
     and white portions)

1 bunch radishes, thinly sliced

To make the vinaigrette: Place vinegar, mustard, garlic, shallots, and sherry in a medium-size metal bowl. Slowly whisk in oils, one at a time, making sure that the dressing is emulsifying. Add salt and pepper to taste. Add the basil. Reserve. This dressing keeps in the refrigerator up to 2 weeks.

To make the salad: Place cooked rice in a medium-size bowl, add julienned peppers, green onions, and radishes. Mix well. Add sherry vinaigrette and toss, making sure to coat the rice thoroughly. Cool until ready to serve.

Serves 4

Marinated Oranges and Strawberries in Grand Marnier and Black Pepper

1 pint strawberries, cleaned and hulled
4 oranges, peel and pith removed
½ cup Grand Marnier
¼ cup sugar
1 teaspoon cracked black pepper
1 teaspoon orange zest

Slice cleaned strawberries in half, or in quarters if they are very large. Place them in a medium-size mixing bowl. Slice oranges very thin and add to the strawberries. In a small bowl, combine Grand Marnier, sugar, pepper, and zest. Mix thoroughly. Toss with strawberries and oranges. Chill until ready to serve.

Serves 4

Sweet Onion Herb Flan

Crust
1¼ cups flour
1 teaspoon salt
¼ cup vegetable shortening
¼ cup unsalted butter
¼ cup ice-cold water

Custard
2 tablespoons vegetable oil
3 medium Walla Walla onions (or yellow or local sweet
*   onions), sliced very thin*
1 cup white wine
1 teaspoon each finely chopped fresh thyme, marjoram, and
*   oregano (reduce to ½ teaspoon if using dried herbs)*
1 cup half-and-half
4 large eggs, slightly beaten
2 ounces mild, soft goat cheese
Salt and pepper to taste

Preheat oven to 425 degrees.

To make the crust: Place flour and salt in a medium-size mixing bowl. Add shortening and butter, and mix to form small beads. Add cold water and stir with a fork just until the dough comes together. Do not overmix. Wrap the dough in plastic wrap and chill for 30 minutes.

Remove the dough from the plastic and roll out to about ¼ inch thick. Place dough loosely in a greased, 10-inch flan pan. Remove excess dough by rolling a rolling pin across the top edge of the pan. Prick with a fork and bake 10 minutes. Cool and reserve.

To make the custard: Lower oven temperature to 350 degrees. Heat oil in a heavy sauté pan until smoking hot. Sauté onions until evenly brown. Add wine, reduce heat to low, and cook until wine has evaporated. Remove from heat and cool.

In a mixing bowl, combine herbs, half-and-half, eggs, goat cheese, and salt and pepper. Mix well.

Spread onions on the bottom of the flan shell. Pour custard mixture over the onions. Bake 30 to 40 minutes or until a knife inserted comes out clean. Cool until ready to serve.

Makes 1 10-inch flan

VARIATIONS: If goat cheese is unavailable, or if you just don't care for it, substitute grated Parmesan or mild Gouda. Place the cheese on the bottom of the crust (then the onions) instead of in the custard.

John's Cured Broiled Salmon

Cure Mix

½ pound kosher salt
1 pound brown sugar
2 tablespoons garlic powder
1 tablespoon ground cloves
2 tablespoons onion powder
2 tablespoons crushed bay leaf
2 tablespoons ground allspice
2 tablespoons ground mace

4 6-ounce salmon fillets
2 tablespoons vegetable oil

To make cure mix: Combine all ingredients for the cure mix and blend thoroughly. Store in an airtight container until ready to use (you can store it up to 1 year).

To cook salmon: Rub the salmon fillets with enough of the cure mix to cover them well. Cure the salmon 2 to 4 hours in a covered container in the refrigerator. Curing time will depend on the size of the fish. For a moister but milder-flavored fish, cure a shorter time. To stop the curing process, rinse the cure off with cold water and brush the fish with vegetable oil. It is ready to grill.

Grill on outdoor barbecue grill (or broil in the oven) to desired doneness, about 5 to 7 minutes for medium rare. Cool until ready to serve.

Serves 4

199

Chocolate Chocolate-Chip Cheesecake Tart

Crust

1 9-ounce box chocolate wafer cookies
½ cup unsalted butter, melted

Batter

6 ounces semisweet chocolate
1 cup sugar
1½ pounds cream cheese, softened
½ teaspoon vanilla
5 large eggs
1 cup semisweet chocolate chips

To make the crust: Crush cookies in a food processor fitted with a metal blade. With the motor running, slowly add the melted butter and process until well mixed. If the mixture seems a bit dry add another tablespoon of melted butter.

Press the cookie mixture into the bottom and sides of a greased 10-inch flan pan, evenly coating the entire pan. Chill for 20 minutes.

Preheat oven to 350 degrees.

Melt semisweet chocolate over a double boiler. Cream the sugar and cream cheese with a mixer or food processor until smooth. Add vanilla and mix again. Add the eggs, one at a time, mixing well after each one. Fold in melted chocolate until well blended, then fold in chocolate chips.

Pour into the crust and bake 25 to 30 minutes, or until a knife inserted comes out clean. Cool until ready to serve.

Makes 1 10-inch flan

VARIATIONS: To give the tart a mocha flavor, add 1 tablespoon of instant coffee, dissolved in 2 tablespoons of hot water, to the cheesecake batter.

PACIFIC RIM LUNCH FOR 6

**Wild Greens with Chicken
and Sorrel Mango Vinaigrette**

**Singing Scallops Poached in Coconut Milk,
Sake, Basil, and Garlic**

**Cantaloupe Sorbet with
Macadamia Butter Cookies**

WINE SUGGESTION
Chinook Sauvignon Blanc

I HAVE ALWAYS BEEN FASCINATED by different people, foods, and traditions. While I've been fortunate to be able to travel abroad, I'm also blessed to live in a city that is ethnically diverse. I am particularly drawn to Asian cultures, which are well represented in Seattle. The importance of both flavor and beauty in Chinese and Thai foods, for example, is apparent in every facet of their cooking. Both emphasize eye appeal, or presentation, in addition to a wide variety of tastes. Their approach has inspired many of my dishes.

This luncheon menu has a distinct Pacific Rim influence. The combination of basil and coconut in the scallop entree comes from Thai cuisine. The salad is made somewhat like an Oriental stir fry, then poured over fresh wild greens. The cookies in this menu use one of the best (and most expensive) of all nuts, the tropical macadamia. Most are produced in Hawaii, but they actually originated in Australia, and were introduced in the Hawaiian Islands in the late 1800s.

You can serve the first two courses together or one at a time, to allow your guests to savor each dish in its entirety. The dishes themselves are also very flexible. You can change any of the salad vegetables to accommodate your own tastes, or add different herbs, such as fresh thyme or tarragon, to the singing scallops.

Singing scallops are becoming very popular in the Northwest. In British Columbia and northern Washington, some aquaculture ventures have begun to grow them. These small, sweet scallops are eaten whole, unlike other scallops, which utilize only the adductor muscle. They are sold in the shell, but because the shell is open even when they're alive, don't use the usual closed-shell criterion for selecting fresh ones. Instead, smell them to be sure they don't have a fishy or ammonia aroma. Before you cook the scallops, be sure to rinse them thoroughly to remove any sand or dirt.

Wild Greens with Chicken and Sorrel Mango Vinaigrette

Vinaigrette

⅓ *cup rice wine vinegar*

1 mango, pureed

Juice of 1 lime

3 shallots, finely chopped

2 garlic cloves, finely chopped

2 teaspoons fresh sorrel

1 teaspoon finely chopped gingerroot

1¼ *cups vegetable oil*

Salt and pepper to taste

Salad

1 tablespoon vegetable oil

3 chicken breasts

1 pound cleaned wild greens

¼ *pound snow peas*

1 daikon, julienned

1 yellow or red bell pepper, julienned

¼ *pound shiitake mushrooms, sliced*

1 red onion, thinly sliced

Pickled ginger for garnish

To make the vinaigrette: In a medium-size mixing bowl place vinegar, mango puree, lime juice, shallots, garlic, sorrel, and ginger. Slowly whisk in oil to emulsify the dressing. Once the oil is incorporated, season with salt and pepper. Refrigerate.

To prepare the salad: Sauté or grill the chicken breasts. To sauté, heat a heavy pan with oil until smoking hot, sear the chicken on both sides, and finish in a 350-degree oven for about 3 to 5 minutes. Cool, slice, and reserve. To grill, lightly oil and season chicken breasts. Cook about 10 minutes on the grill, or until done.

Place wild greens and vegetables in a large mixing bowl. Add dressing and toss. Place salad on plates and arrange the sliced chicken on top of the greens. Garnish with pickled ginger.

Serves 6

Singing Scallops Poached in Coconut Milk, Sake, Basil, and Garlic

3 pounds singing scallops (or mussels)
¼ cup coconut milk
1 cup sake
4 shallots, finely chopped
5 garlic cloves, finely chopped
1 tablespoon finely chopped fresh basil
Salt and pepper to taste

Steamed rice (optional)

Rinse scallops well and place in a 5-quart stockpot. Add the remaining ingredients (except rice), cover, place over high heat, and bring to a boil. Steam about 5 to 7 minutes, or until the scallops are easily removed from the shell.

Remove scallops from the liquid and transfer to individual bowls. Return stockpot to high heat and reduce the poaching liquid by half. Season with salt and pepper and pour over the scallops. Serve immediately with steamed rice on the side.

205

Serves 6

Cantaloupe Sorbet

2 cantaloupes, peeled and pureed
¾ cup sugar
¼ cup water
2 egg whites, slightly beaten (foamy)

Fresh mint sprigs for garnish

Place cantaloupe puree in a medium-size metal bowl and reserve. In a small heavy sauté pan, bring sugar and water to a boil. Remove sugar mixture from heat and stir into the puree. Fold in egg whites that have been slightly beaten (until foamy) and place the bowl in the freezer.

Every 30 minutes, take the sorbet out of the freezer and stir it. The more you stir the sorbet, the smoother it will be when frozen. Do this until the sorbet is as smooth as you want it. I suggest you stir it at least 4 times, but you can continue the process much longer.

Serve in chilled bowls and garnish with fresh mint.

206

Serves 6

Macadamia Butter Cookies

1 cup unsalted butter, softened
¾ cup powdered sugar
½ cup ground unsalted macadamias
1 teaspoon orange zest
1⅓ cups flour
1 teaspoon salt

Preheat oven to 350 degrees.

With a mixer set on medium speed, cream butter and sugar until fluffy. Add nuts and orange zest and mix for another 2 minutes. On slow speed, add flour in 3 parts. Once the flour is incorporated, add salt and mix again.

Wrap cookie dough in plastic wrap and refrigerate for 30 minutes. When chilled, roll the dough out to ¼ inch thick on a well-floured surface. Using a cookie cutter, cut out desired shapes. Bake on a greased cookie sheet for 10 minutes, or until golden brown. Cool on a wire rack and store well covered.

207

Makes about 2 dozen cookies

VARIATIONS: Try these cookies with other types of nuts and spices like ½ teaspoon nutmeg or 1 teaspoon cinnamon.

NOTE: If the dough becomes too soft, return to refrigerator for another 10 minutes.

Tomato Tart and Endive Salad
Luncheon for 4

Grilled Endive Salad

Tomato and Basil Tart

Apricot Streusel Flan

WINE SUGGESTION
Fetzer Reserve Pinot Noir

LATE SUMMER, WHEN TOMATOES are ripening on the vine, I go tomato crazy. Last year in our garden, we had two Early Girl tomato plants, which started producing in August—and produced, and produced, and produced. I couldn't keep up with them. I took to eating them straight from the plant while working in the yard.

This summer menu uses these beauties with another summer jewel in a classic combination—big, red, gorgeous, vine-ripened tomatoes and aromatic, fresh basil. I've added no more to these gems than a bit of fresh ricotta, Italian parsley, and a simple butter crust to make a fresh garden tart. Serve at room temperature to really bring out the flavors, and if there is any left over, polish it off at breakfast the next morning.

The grilled endive salad is a great way to eat the sometimes bitter Belgian endive and radicchio. Marinating the endive for a half hour or so, then grilling it over a hot flame helps to remove the bitterness. The tarragon in the vinaigrette adds just a bit of licorice flavor to the salad, which is enhanced by tarragon vinegar and the richness of the balsamic vinegar. This salad is best made the day before and served at room temperature.

Dessert features sweet apricots, which in Washingon State are grown mostly in the Yakima Valley. The fruit is layered with sour cream that is sweetened with a little sugar, and then placed on a rich tart dough, flavored with rum and brown sugar. A streusel dough enriched with almonds tops the tart. A nice touch with this recipe would be to make individual tartlets, each with half an apricot.

Grilled Endive Salad

2 heads radicchio
4 heads Belgian endive
2 shallots, finely chopped
3 garlic cloves, finely chopped
1 teaspoon finely chopped fresh tarragon
2 tablespoons tarragon wine vinegar
2 tablespoons balsamic vinegar
¾ cup extra virgin olive oil
1 teaspoon cracked black pepper
Salt to taste

1 red bell pepper, julienned, for garnish
2 sprigs fresh tarragon for garnish

Quarter radicchio heads and remove cores. Split endive heads in half and place in a large mixing bowl with quartered radicchio.

In a small mixing bowl, combine all other ingredients (except garnish) and mix well. Pour over endive and radicchio and allow to stand 30 minutes.

Remove radicchio and endive from the bowl, draining dressing back into the bowl, and grill on a hot ungreased grill until lightly browned. Allow to cool, then julienne. Return julienned radicchio and endive to bowl with dressing and toss until well mixed.

Distribute on salad plates and garnish with julienned red pepper and fresh tarragon sprigs. Serve at room temperature.

Serves 4

Tomato and Basil Tart

Crust

2 cups flour
1 bulb Roasted Garlic (see page 229), cloves peeled
Pinch of salt
1 cup unsalted butter

Filling

¾ cup grated Parmesan cheese
1 bunch fresh basil, chopped
1 cup ricotta cheese
1 teaspoon chopped Italian parsley
2 egg yolks
½ teaspoon salt
8 vine-ripened Roma tomatoes, thinly sliced

Preheat oven to 350 degrees.

To make the crust: In a food processor fitted with a metal blade, place flour and cloves of Roasted Garlic. While the machine is running, add the salt, then slowly add butter. Process until the dough forms a ball. Stop machine and remove dough. Press onto bottom and sides of a greased 12-inch flan pan. Bake crust about 10 minutes (do not let brown). Remove from oven and cool.

To make the filling: Sprinkle ½ cup of the Parmesan cheese on the bottom of the baked crust. Cover with chopped basil. In a small mixing bowl, mix together ricotta cheese, parsley, egg yolks, and salt. Spread the ricotta mixture over the basil, then cover with sliced tomatoes. Top tart with remaining Parmesan cheese.

Bake 20 to 25 minutes, until cheese is melted and golden brown. Cool, then remove from pan. Serve warm.

Makes 1 12-inch tart

211

Apricot Streusel Flan

Crust

2 cups flour

½ cup brown sugar

½ teaspoon vanilla

2 tablespoons rum extract

½ teaspoon salt

1 cup unsalted butter

Filling

10 ripe apricots, peeled and halved

¾ cup sour cream

⅓ cup powdered sugar

1 tablespoon rum extract

3 egg yolks

Topping

1 cup flour

¼ cup ground toasted almonds

½ cup butter, softened

Preheat oven to 350 degrees.

To make the crust: In a food processor fitted with a metal blade, place flour, brown sugar, vanilla, rum extract, and salt. Process slowly. Add butter and allow machine to run until dough forms a ball. Remove from food processor bowl and press onto bottom and sides of a greased 12-inch flan pan. Bake 10 minutes (do not allow to brown). Cool.

To make the filling: Arrange apricots on the crust in concentric circles. In a small mixing bowl, combine sour cream, powdered sugar, rum extract, and egg yolks. Mix well and pour over apricots.

To make the topping: In a small bowl, combine flour and almonds. Add softened butter and mix until it forms a

crumbly dough. Sprinkle topping over apricot mixture and
bake flan for about 25 to 30 minutes, or until topping is
golden brown. Serve warm or cool.

Makes 1 12-inch flan

SMOKED TROUT AND SPINACH FETTUCCINE BRUNCH FOR 6

Melon Salad

Smoked Trout and Spinach
Tossed with Egg Fettuccine

Herb Buttermilk Muffins

WHAT I CONSIDER BREAKFAST time is really brunch for most people. But eating late allows me freedom in designing breakfast menus. Every so often, a bit of lunch nudges into my breakfast, like it does in this one, with its combination of pasta, melon and prosciutto salad, and herb muffins.

While developing this brunch menu, I was thinking what a great dinner it would make. When I was a kid, my mother made breakfast dinners every so often. I loved them because I was never awake enough in the morning to enjoy breakfast. Some things never change.

The first course combines three different melons tossed with a sweet sherry, prosciutto, and mint. This is my variation on melon slices wrapped in prosciutto. Buy melons that are sweet and juicy, and a good-quality prosciutto, because you are using only a small amount and you need maximum flavor. Also, since the sherry isn't cooked out of this dish, use a good-quality sherry.

The pasta dish combines the flavors of mild, smoked trout with tender spinach, marjoram, and oregano, topped with a bit of Romano cheese and tangy capers. This dish should be completed just before serving, but most of the preparation can be done ahead. If you do cook the pasta before putting the dish together, coat it with olive oil. The eggs added to the pasta thicken the sauce and should be handled quickly and off the stove so that they don't overcook.

To accompany the dishes, I have devised a muffin recipe rich in herbs and Parmesan cheese, with just a touch of buttermilk. These muffins go great with all kinds of soups, warm and cold salads, and scrambled eggs.

Melon Salad

1 medium cantaloupe, peeled and diced medium
1 medium honeydew melon, peeled and diced medium
1 medium Crenshaw melon, peeled and diced medium
½ cup sweet sherry
¼ pound prosciutto, julienned
½ teaspoon finely chopped fresh mint

Radicchio leaves and fresh mint sprigs for garnish

Place melon cubes in a large bowl and toss together. Add sherry, julienned prosciutto, and chopped mint. Allow to sit at room temperature 1 hour before serving. Place on serving platter lined with radicchio leaves, and garnish with fresh mint sprigs.

Serves 6

Smoked Trout and Spinach Tossed with Egg Fettuccine

2 quarts water
1 teaspoon salt
Splash of olive oil
1½ pounds fresh egg fettuccine

1 pound boneless smoked trout

3 shallots, finely chopped
3 garlic cloves, finely chopped
3 tablespoons unsalted butter
1 bunch spinach leaves, washed
½ teaspoon finely chopped fresh marjoram
½ teaspoon finely chopped fresh oregano
1½ cups heavy cream
3 egg yolks, slightly beaten
½ cup grated Romano cheese
1 teaspoon capers
Salt and pepper to taste

Sprigs of fresh herbs (marjoram, oregano, or Italian parsley)
*   for garnish*

In a large saucepan, bring 2 quarts of water to a boil with salt and olive oil. Add fettuccine and cook about 3 to 4 minutes, just until water returns to a boil. Strain pasta and toss with a bit of olive oil so it doesn't stick together. Reserve.

Flake the smoked trout and reserve.

In a large sauté pan on high heat, sauté shallots and garlic in butter just until you can smell the aroma. Add spinach leaves and sauté until just wilted. Add marjoram, oregano, and cream and cook until the cream starts to thicken. Add fettuccine and toss until coated. Remove pan from the heat and quickly stir in egg yolks, then stir in ¼ cup of the Romano cheese, the smoked trout, and the capers.

Arrange on plates or in a large serving dish. Top with reserved ¼ cup of Romano cheese and sprigs of fresh herbs.

Serves 6

VARIATIONS: Try other cheeses in this dish, such as Gouda and herbed double-cream cheese. Other types of smoked fish, such as smoked salmon and smoked black cod, are great in this dish.

Herb Buttermilk Muffins

1½ cups flour
½ cup whole wheat flour
2 teaspoons baking powder
2 teaspoons sugar
½ teaspooon salt
1 egg
1 cup buttermilk
¼ cup butter, melted
2 tablespoons chopped oregano
2 tablespoons chopped thyme
Dash of Tabasco sauce
¼ cup Parmesan cheese

Preheat oven to 350 degrees.

Combine flours, baking powder, sugar, and salt in a large mixing bowl. In a small mixing bowl, combine egg, buttermilk, butter, oregano, thyme, and Tabasco sauce. Stir into flour mixture just until mixed. Fold in Parmesan cheese.

Pour into greased muffin tins and bake 20 to 25 minutes, or until browned. Serve warm with butter.

Makes 1 dozen muffins

219

Sweet Cornmeal Cakes

Berry Butter

Caramelized Peaches

BESIDES BEING A POTATO FAN, I love breads—any kind, any shape. When I'm asked what I would like for breakfast, I usually say pancakes or waffles. The pancakes in this breakfast have finely ground cornmeal and a bit of sugar and are topped with fresh berry butter and caramelized peaches.

The cornmeal cakes are made a lot like a traditional pancake, except that the eggs are separated and the whites are beaten to stiff peaks, then folded in, to make the cakes very fluffy. Nobody wants to start off a great summer day feeling like a ton of bricks. The cornmeal in these cakes is very finely ground, so it adds just a bit of sweet corn taste and texture, without making them heavy and dense. The cornmeal cakes are served with rosettes of berry butter and caramelized peaches. You can also sprinkle about ⅓ pound of julienned black forest ham over cornmeal cakes before topping them off with the peaches and butter. These cakes make a great dessert when topped with vanilla ice cream and a warm berry compote instead of the fruit butter.

If you like to put up fresh fruit in the summer, make the berry butter while berries are in season and freeze them. In those cold months of winter, they'll remind you of summer. You can also use any berry you like in these butters—I like to use blueberries and marionberries.

The caramelized peaches that top off the cakes are made almost the same way as in the tart recipe in the Caramelized Peach Flan. They are a rather decadent addition to breakfast, but peaches are only ripe for a little while and breakfast, I've heard it said, is the most important meal of the day. Aren't these reasons enough to treat yourself on a beautiful summer morning?

Sweet Cornmeal Cakes

¾ cup flour
½ cup fine cornmeal
2 teaspoons baking powder
¼ cup sugar
2 eggs, separated
1⅓ cups milk
3 tablespoons plus 1 teaspoon vegetable oil
¾ teaspoon salt

In a large bowl, combine flour, cornmeal, baking powder, and sugar. In a small bowl, combine egg yolks, milk, 3 tablespoons oil and salt. Stir in just until flour is moist. In another bowl, whip egg whites until stiff peaks form. Gently fold egg whites into batter.

Grease a griddle or sauté pan with 1 teaspoon of oil, and set over medium heat. When the griddle is hot, pour in about ¼ cup of batter for each cake, making a few at a time. Fry until cakes start to bubble and set. Flip and brown on other side.

Keep cakes warm in the oven until served.

Serves 4

Berry Butter

¼ cup raspberries, washed
¼ cup blackberries, washed
¼ cup powdered sugar
½ teaspoon orange zest
Pinch of nutmeg
Dash of vanilla
½ pound unsalted butter, softened

Place berries, sugar, orange zest, nutmeg, and vanilla in a food processor fitted with a metal blade. Process until berries are pureed. Stop the machine and add softened butter. Process until butter is completely mixed with berries.

Place berry butter in a small pastry bag fitted with a star tube. Pipe rosettes of butter onto a cookie sheet lined with parchment paper. Refrigerate until butter sets. Serve on cracked ice.

Makes 1 cup

HINT: You can freeze leftover butter rosettes on parchment on the cookie sheet. Transfer to covered containers to store in freezer.

Caramelized Peaches

1½ cups sugar
½ cup water
4 peaches, peeled, pitted, and halved
¼ cup brandy

In a very large sauté pan, combine sugar and water. Over high heat, allow mixture to caramelize to a light brown. Place peaches in sugar, cut side up. Reduce heat to medium and brown peaches, cooking until tender. Remove peaches from pan, reserving caramelized sugar, and place on a serving tray.

Pour brandy into caramelized sugar and cook 2 or 3 more minutes on high heat. Pour brandy-sugar mixture over peaches and serve.

Serves 4

BASICS

Fish or Shrimp Stock

2 pounds halibut or other whitefish bones,
        or shells from about 5 pounds of shrimp
1 tablespoon unsalted butter
3 stalks celery, coarsely chopped
1 leek, white only, coarsely chopped
3 shallots, chopped
2 garlic cloves, chopped
1 cup dry white wine
1 bay leaf
2 stems each of thyme, oregano, or marjoram

To make fish stock: Place fish bones, roughly chopped, into a large bowl or pot and cover with cold water. Let the bones soak for 1 to 2 hours.

In a large stockpot, heat butter until melted. Add all the vegetables and sauté lightly. Add bones and wine, cover, and cook 10 minutes. Fill the stockpot with enough water to cover the bones (about 2 quarts). Add bay leaf and herb stems. Simmer 25 to 30 minutes.

To make shrimp stock: Brown the shrimp shells in an ungreased pan in a 350-degree oven just until they turn pink (about 10 minutes). Continue as in fish stock, substituting shrimp shells for fish bones.

Makes 1 quart

NOTE: To obtain a clear stock, be sure to always start with cold water and do not boil the stock. Soaking the bones removes any remaining blood and produces a clearer, better-tasting stock.

Chicken or Duck Stock

2 pounds chicken or duck bones, rinsed
2 large carrots, coarsely chopped
3 stalks celery, coarsely chopped
1 large onion, coarsely chopped
1 bay leaf
2 thyme stems
2 cloves garlic, chopped

To make chicken stock: Place rinsed chicken bones and remaining ingredients in a large stockpot, cover with 2 quarts cold water, and bring to a boil. Reduce heat and simmer 4 to 6 hours, or until the stock has good color and flavor. Strain and keep well covered. Will keep 1 week in the refrigerator.

To make duck stock: In a sauté pan over high heat, brown duck bones. Remove bones from fat (they will produce fat as they brown). Continue for chicken stock.

Makes 1 quart

227

HINT: Place stock into ice cube trays and freeze. Remove frozen cubes from the trays, separate into smaller quantities, and place in freezer bags. When stock is needed, you don't have to thaw more stock than you need.

Veal Stock

2 pounds veal bones, rinsed
2 tablespoons vegetable oil
2 carrots, coarsely chopped
3 stalks celery, coarsely chopped
1 large onion, coarsely chopped
3 cloves garlic, chopped
2 tablespoons tomato paste
½ cup red wine
2 stems thyme (or 2 stems oregano or marjoram)

Heat oven to 500 degrees. Place a large roasting pan in the oven with vegetable oil and heat until smoking hot. Place bones in pan and roast until golden. Add vegetables and continue browning. When vegetables are almost browned, add tomato paste and mix to coat bones and vegetables. Cook another 5 to 10 minutes to slightly brown the tomato paste.

Remove pan from oven. Using a slotted spoon, transfer bones and vegetables to a large stockpot. Drain oil from roasting pan, then pour wine into pan and scrape drippings. Transfer wine and drippings to the stockpot with the bones. Add 2 quarts cold water and bring to a boil. Lower heat to simmer. Cook 6 to 8 hours, or until the stock has a good rich color.

Makes 1 quart

Roasted Garlic

2 large bulbs garlic
¼ cup vegetable oil

Heat oven to 250 degrees. Cut the tops off garlic bulbs, about ¼ inch from the top. Place garlic in a heavy, ovenproof sauté pan with the vegetable oil and put in oven. Roast until garlic bulbs are very soft, about 40 minutes. Reserve, keeping the garlic warm until ready to serve or use in recipes.

Remove individual cloves from the head with a fork.

Oven Roasted Shallots

6 shallots
2 tablespoons vegetable oil

Heat oven to 250 degrees. Place whole shallots and oil in heavy, ovenproof sauté pan. Roast until shallots are very soft, about 40 minutes.

Simple Syrup

1 cup sugar
2 cups water
1 teaspoon lemon zest
1 teaspoon orange zest

In a heavy pan, place sugar and water. Cook over high heat until sugar dissolves. Add lemon and orange zest and cook until mixture comes to a boil. Remove from heat and strain. Keep covered and refrigerate up to 1 month.

Makes about 1 pint

Crème Fraîche

1 cup heavy cream
1 teaspoon sour cream

Place cream and sour cream in a small bowl and mix well. Cover and let stand at room temperature overnight, then refrigerate. The mixture will become very thick once chilled.

Makes 1 cup

Candied Orange Peel

2 tablespoons water
½ cup sugar
Peel from 1 orange, cut into very thin strips

Bring water and sugar to a boil until sugar is dissolved, about 2 to 3 minutes. Toss in orange peel. Cook about 2 more minutes, until nice and coated. Remove from heat and pull out peel with a slotted spoon. Drain on parchment paper or waxed paper and cool.

231

Terms and Techniques

Dice To cut into cubes. A small dice is a ¼-inch cube, medium is approximately ⅓ inch, and large is approximately ¾ inch.

Edible flowers There are about 120 different edible flowers, including pansies, petunias, Johnny-jump-ups, violas, calendulas, and fuschias. They can be used as garnish or added to salads.

Emulsify To suspend acid in a fat, in forms such as mayonnaise or hollandaise sauce, by breaking up the fat molecules through whisking or beating.

Incorporate To mix in thoroughly.

Julienne A cut approximately ⅛ inch by 2 inches (or shorter), about the size of a matchstick.

Mignonette A sauce often used with oysters, with a base of wine and vinegar.

Mince To finely chop.

Poach To cook in a clear, spiced, or flavored stock.

Reduce To thicken a sauce by boiling out the liquid. This method requires very little stirring because the action of the reduction mixes the liquid.

Sabayon A foamy dessert sauce with an egg yolk base.

Sauce When serving, to place the sauce either over or underneath the entree.

Steam To cook with a small amount of liquid at high heat.

Toasted nuts To toast raw nuts, place in a heavy fry pan or sauté pan over medium heat for several minutes. Stir occasionally. They should be just starting to brown a bit. When toasting hazelnuts, the skin will begin to blister and peel when done.

237

239